SPORTING FIREARMS

A CLASSIC HANDBOOK ON HUNTING TOOLS, MARKSMANSHIP, AND ESSENTIAL EQUIPMENT FOR THE FIELD

BY **HORACE KEPHART**

ORIGINALLY PUBLISHED IN 1912

LEGACY EDITION

THE CLASSIC OUTING HANDBOOKS COLLECTION

BOOK 16

FEATURING

REMASTERED CLASSIC WORKS OF THE HIGHEST QUALITY FROM **THE TIMELESS MASTERS AND TEACHERS** OF TRADITIONAL HANDCRAFTS AND OUTDOORS SKILLS

Doublebit Press

New content, introduction, cover design, and annotations Copyright © 2020 by Doublebit Press. All rights reserved.

Doublebit Press is an imprint of Eagle Nest Press www.doublebitpress.com | Cherry, IL, USA

Originally published in 1912 by Horace Kephart.

This title, along with other Doublebit Press books are available at a volume discount for youth groups, outdoors clubs, craft groups, or reading groups. Contact us at info@doublebitpress.com for more information.

*Doublebit Press Legacy Edition ISBNs
Hardcover: 978-1-64389-172-9
Paperback: 978-1-64389-173-6*

Part of the Classic Outing Handbooks Collection: Book 16

Disclaimer: Because of its age and historic context, this text could contain content on present-day inappropriate outdoors activities, outdated medical information, unsafe chemical and mechanical processes, or culturally and racially insensitive content. Doublebit Press, or its employees, authors, and other affiliates, assume no liability for any actions performed by readers or any damages that might be related to information contained in this book. This text has been published for historical study and for personal literary enrichment toward the goal of the preservation of American outdoors and handcraft history and heritage.

First Doublebit Press Legacy Edition Printing, 2020

INTRODUCTION
To The Doublebit Press Legacy Edition

The old experts of the woods, mountains, and farm country life taught timeless principles and skills for decades. Through their books, the old experts offered rich descriptions of the outdoor world and encouraged learning through personal experiences in nature. Over the last 125 years, handcrafts, artisanal works, outdoors activities, and our experiences with nature have substantially changed. Many things have gotten simpler as equipment and processes have improved, and life outside, on the farm, or on the trail now brings with it many of the same comforts enjoyed in town. In addition, some activities of the old days are now no longer in vogue, or are even outright considered inappropriate or illegal. However, despite many of the positive changes in handcrafting, traditional skills, and outdoors methods that have occurred over the years, *there are many other skills and much knowledge that are at risk of being lost* that should never be forgotten.

By publishing Legacy Editions of classic texts on handcrafts, artisanal skills, nature lore, survival, and outdoors and camping life, it is our goal at Doublebit Press to do what we can to preserve and share the works from forgotten teachers that form the cornerstone of the authentic and hard-wrought American tradition of self-sustainability and self-reliance. Through remastered reprint editions of timeless classics of traditional crafts, classic methods, and outdoor recreation, perhaps we can regain some of this lost knowledge for future generations.

On the frontier, folks made virtually everything by hand. Old farmers' knowledge and homestead skills were passed on to the future generation because it meant survival. In addition, much of traditional handcrafts and outdoors life knowledge was passed on from American Indians – the original handcrafters and outdoorsmen of the Americas.

Today, much of the handcrafted items of the frontier are made in factories, only briefly seeing a human during the process (if at all). Making things by hand indeed takes much (often strenuous) work, but it provides an extreme sense of pride in the finished job. Instantly, all hand-made items come with a story on their creation. Most importantly, though, making items with traditional methods gives you experience and knowledge of how things work.

This is similar to the case of camping and the modern outdoors experience, with neatly arranged campsites at public campgrounds and camping gear that has been meticulously improved and tested in both the lab and the field. These changes have also caused us to lose this traditional knowledge, having it buried in the latest high-tech iteration of your latest camp gadget.

Many modern conveniences are only a brief trek away, with many parks, campgrounds, and even forests having easy-access roads, convenience stores, and even cell phone signal. In some ways, it is much easier to camp and go outdoors today, and that is a good thing! We should not be miserable when we go outside — lovers of the outdoors know the essential restorative capability that the woods can have on the body, mind, and soul. But to experience it, you need to not be surrounded by modern high-tech robotic coffee pots, tents that build themselves, or watches that tell you how to do everything!

Although things have gotten easier on us in the 21st Century when it comes to handcrafts and the outdoors, it certainly does not mean that we should forget the foundations of technical skills, artisanal production, and outdoors lore. All of the modern tools and cool gizmos that make our lives easier are all founded on principles of traditional methods that the old masters knew well and taught to those who would listen. We just have to look deeply into the design of our modern gadgets and factories to see the original methods and traditional skills at play.

Every woods master and artisan had their own curriculum or thought some things were more important than others. The old masters also taught common things in slightly different ways or did things differently than others. That's what makes each of the experts different and worth reading. There's no universal way of doing something, especially today. Learning to go about something differently helps with mastery or learn a new skill altogether. Basically, you learn intimately how things work, giving you great skill with adapting and being flexible when the need arises.

Again, to use the metaphor from the above paragraphs, traditional skills mastery consists of learning the basic building blocks of how and why the old artisans made things, how they lived outdoors, and why woods and nature lore mattered. Everything is intertwined, and doing it by hand increases your knowledge of this complex network. Each master goes about describing these building blocks differently or shows a different aspect of them.

Therefore, we have decided to publish this Legacy Edition reprint in our collection of traditional handcraft and outdoors life classics. This book is an important contribution to the early American traditional skills and outdoors literature, and has important historical and collector value toward preserving the American tradition of self-sufficiency and artisan production. The knowledge it holds is an invaluable reference for practicing outdoors skills and hand craft methods. Its chapters thoroughly discuss some of the essential building blocks of knowledge that are fundamental but may have been forgotten as equipment gets fancier and technology gets smarter. In short, this book was chosen for Legacy Edition printing because much of the basic skills and knowledge it contains has been forgotten or put to the wayside in trade for more modern conveniences and methods.

Although the editors at Doublebit Press are thrilled to have comfortable experiences in the woods and love our modern equipment for making cool hand-made projects, we are also realizing that the basic skills taught by the old masters are more essential than ever as our culture becomes more and more hooked on digital stuff. We don't want to risk forgetting the important steps, skills, or building blocks involved with each step of traditional methods. Sometimes, *there's no substitute for just doing something on your own, by hand.* Sometimes, to truly learn something is to *just do it by hand.* The Legacy Edition series represents the essential contributions to the American handcraft and outdoors tradition by the great experts.

With technology playing a major role in everyday life, sometimes we need to take a step back in time to find those basic building blocks used for gaining mastery – the things that we have luckily not completely lost and has been recorded in books over the last two centuries. These skills aren't forgotten, they've just been shelved. *It's time to unshelve them once again and reclaim the lost knowledge of self-sufficiency.*

Based on this commitment to preserving our outdoors and handcraft heritage, we have taken great pride in publishing this book as a complete original work without any editorial changes or revisions. We hope it is worthy of both study and collection by handcrafters and outdoors folk in the modern era and to fulfill its status as a Legacy Edition by passing along to the libraries of future generations.

Unlike many other low-resolution photocopy reproductions of classic books that are common on the market, this Legacy Edition does not simply place poor photography of old texts on our pages and use error-prone optical scanning or computer-generated text. We want our work to speak for itself and reflect the quality demanded by our customers who spend their hard-earned money. With this in mind, each Legacy Edition book that has been chosen for publication is carefully remastered from original print books, *with the Doublebit Legacy Edition printed and laid out in the exact way that it was presented at its original publication.* Our Legacy Edition books are inspired by the original covers of first-edition texts, embracing the beauty that is in both the simplicity and sometimes ornate decoration of vintage and antique books. We want provide a beautiful, memorable experience that is as true to the original text as best as possible, but with the aid of modern technology to make as meaningful a reading experience as possible for books that are typically over a century old.

Because of its age and because it is presented in its original form, the book may contain misspellings, inking errors, and other print blemishes that were common for the age. However, these are exactly the things that we feel give the book its character, which we preserved in this Legacy Edition. During digitization, we did our best to ensure that each illustration in the text was clean and sharp with the least amount of loss from being copied and digitized as possible. Full-page plate illustrations are presented as they were found, often including the extra blank page that was often behind a plate and plate pagination. For the covers, we use the original cover design as our template to give the book its original feel. We are sure you'll appreciate the fine touches and attention to detail that your Legacy Edition has to offer.

For traditional handcrafters and outdoors enthusiasts who demand the best from their equipment, this Doublebit Press Legacy Edition reprint was made with you in mind. Both important and minor details have equally both been accounted for by our publishing staff, down to the cover, font, layout, and images. It is the goal of Doublebit Legacy Edition series to preserve America's handcrafting and outdoors heritage, but also be cherished as collectible pieces, worthy of collection in any person's library and that can be passed to future generations.

Every book selected to be in this series offers unique views and instruction on important skills, advice, tips, tidbits, anecdotes, stories, and experiences that will enrich the repertoire of any person looking to learn the skills it contains. To learn the most basic building blocks leads to mastery of all its aspects.

SPORTING FIREARMS

SPORTING FIREARMS

BY

HORACE KEPHART

AUTHOR OF "THE BOOK OF CAMPING AND
WOODCRAFT," "CAMP COOKERY," ETC.

Illustrated with Diagrams

NEW YORK
OUTING PUBLISHING COMPANY
MCMXII

COPYRIGHT, 1912, BY
OUTING PUBLISHING COMPANY.

Entered at Stationer's Hall, London, England.
All rights reserved

FOREWORD

It is assumed that the reader of this booklet is familiar with gun catalogues—hence space is saved by omitting nearly everything that catalogues have to say.

Let us consider rifles and shotguns from the user's standpoint, simply as tools of sport, to be judged strictly on their merits. The "make" of a gun, like a horse's pedigree, may be of good or ill repute; but it is not a final guarantee of merit.

To prove a gun thoroughly, it must be tested both on the range and in the field. Nobody can tell from field shooting alone just what a gun's shooting qualities are; nor can anybody tell much about its killing power and serviceability until he has used it a good deal on game.

HORACE KEPHART.

Bryson, N. C. January, 1912.

TABLE OF CONTENTS

CHAPTER PAGE
- I. RIFLES AND AMMUNITION 11
- II. THE FLIGHT OF BULLETS 26
- III. KILLING POWER 40
- IV. RIFLE MECHANISM AND MATERIALS 59
- V. RIFLE SIGHTS 76
- VI. TRIGGERS AND STOCKS — CARE OF RIFLE 91

PART II. THE SHOTGUN

- VII. SHOT PATTERNS AND PENETRATION 109
- VIII. GAUGES AND WEIGHTS 124
- IX. MECHANISM AND BUILD OF SHOTGUNS 140

SPORTING FIREARMS

SPORTING FIREARMS

CHAPTER I

RIFLES AND AMMUNITION

THE shooting merits of a rifle are rated by the accuracy, velocity, and force with which it delivers bullets. I use the word force, for brevity's sake, in an arbitrary sense, to include energy of impact, penetration, and shock.

Some rifles are accurate, but drive the bullets so slowly that they describe a high curve, so that they will over-shoot or under-shoot beyond, say, fifty yards, unless the distance is closely estimated and proper allowance is made in aiming. Some shoot swift and hard, but drive their bullets now high, now low, now right, now left, and no man can tell just where they will hit. Others shoot swift, and hard, and true: they can be relied upon to hit " where they are held," without allowing for distance, up to, say, one hundred and fifty yards. When all three merits are combined in the same gun we have a weapon of high ballistic

SPORTING FIREARMS

efficiency—an "old reliable" that a man may well be proud of.

I have spoken in hunters' terms and as though it were the gun alone that did the work. But the degree of accuracy, velocity, and force with which a rifle shoots is really determined not so much by the weapon itself as by the charge with which it is loaded. If a novice should ask "How straight and how hard does a Winchester rifle shoot?" (or a Remington, or any other) nobody could give a direct answer; for it depends on what cartridge is used. If, on the other hand, he should ask "How straight and how hard does a .25-35 Winchester cartridge shoot?" (or any other) we could answer definitely; for it will give about the same results in any standard arm that is made to use it.

Of course, the precision with which a bullet *starts* on its errand is governed largely by the design, material, and mechanical perfection of the gun barrel. So, too, velocity of bullet depends somewhat upon length of barrel. But the common experience of gunmakers has so nearly standardized these matters that we need not consider them for the present.

The cartridge determines the kind of work that a rifle can do. It is a law of scientific gunnery

RIFLES AND AMMUNITION

to design first a cartridge, then a gun to handle it. And this is done in practical gunmaking whenever an arm of superior ballistics is produced. On the contrary, whenever a charge is ill-balanced or a bullet malformed, for the sake of fitting the cartridge to a particular breech mechanism, bad shooting is bound to result.

This matter is so important, yet so commonly overlooked, that I may be allowed a little space to illustrate and emphasize it:

In the half-century preceding our Civil War the muzzle-loader reached its highest development. After infinitely varied experiments, American riflemen discovered a peculiar bullet called the "sugar loaf" (*fig. 1*) that outclassed all

FIGURE 1.

others in ballistic merit. Its length was a little less than twice its own caliber. Its distinguishing feature was an extremely slow taper from point to base, the bearing or cylindrical part being so short that this bullet could only be loaded by using a false muzzle to start it. Except for a slightly blunted tip, it had fine lines, like a boat

SPORTING FIREARMS

built for high speed. It flew with extreme accuracy up to five hundred yards, and with a lower curve or trajectory than any other form of conical ball.

With such bullets a rifle by Morgan James made a score of twenty-five consecutive shots, at two hundred and twenty yards, with average deviation of 1.4 inch; also ten shots, same distance, average deviation .8 inch, measuring from center of bullet hole to center of group (targets published in *Atlantic Monthly*, October, 1859). The bullet here illustrated was used, in a .42-130-270 muzzle-loader, in the *Forest and Stream* trajectory test at Creedmoor in 1885, and made a lower curve than any American or foreign breech-loader of its day (height of trajectory 6.4 inches midway over the two hundred yard range). We may say that this or a similar charge gave the highest ballistic efficiency—the best combination of accuracy, velocity, and force—that ever was attained with black gunpowder within sporting ranges.

When breech-loaders were introduced the sugar-loaf bullet could not be used in them, owing to its short bearing. Their mechanism was so weak, and the shells were so weak, that breech pressure had to be kept down to a low figure.

RIFLES AND AMMUNITION

This could only be done by using a small charge of powder and a light, short bullet. Still, the bullet had to have considerable bearing, in order to start straight.

This meant a bluff shoulder, like the bow of a canal boat, and consequent low speed. Such a bullet is illustrated in *fig. 2*, the well known .44-

FIGURE 2.

40-200. The accuracy of such a charge is far inferior to the one previously mentioned. Its trajectory is so high (sixteen inches midway over the two hundred yard range) that shooting it beyond one hundred yards is mostly guesswork, and seldom effective. And yet more of this ammunition, probably, was sold in America than any other that has been used on big game, and more game has been killed with it than with any other. It came into use at the right time, when an army of hunters, many of them ex-soldiers, advanced into the West, where game was wonderfully plentiful. These cartridges were cheap, and they could be bought at any frontier post. Game was easily approached, in those days, and sportsmanship

SPORTING FIREARMS

had no more ethics than timber cutting—nobody cared how many broken-legged or gut-shot animals crawled off to fester miserably in a thicket and die by slow torture.

So it came to pass that the record for American game shooting was won by as poor a cartridge as ever was forced into an arbitrary shape. It should be noted, in this case, that the bullet is of only 1½ calibers length, cylindrical throughout half its length, and very blunt. Such a missile will fly straight enough to satisfy average men, up to one hundred and fifty yards, if started at very slow speed (standard muzzle velocity 1,300 feet a second). If driven by a strong charge of powder it would meet excessive air resistance, would waste energy like a bluff-bowed boat driven by powerful engines, would " corkscrew " in its flight, and soon would go staggering like a ship without a rudder.

Good marksmen never were satisfied with such ammunition as the .44-40, .38-40, .32-20, and others similarly proportioned. The demand for something more accurate and of surer killing power became insistent. It was met by a series of cartridges of radically different type, in which the bullet was of from 2½ to 3 calibers length, such as the .45-110-550, .45-70-405, .40-90-370,

RIFLES AND AMMUNITION

.40-70-330, .38-55-255, and .32-40-165. (The first figure, in each case, is the caliber in hundredths of an inch; the second is the weight of powder, in grains; the third is the weight of bullet, in grains.) The .45-70-405 bullet is shown, as an example in *fig. 3*.

FIGURE 3.

These were the most accurate sporting cartridges produced in black powder days. Their bullets, being long and heavy, could only be driven at low speed (1,300 to 1,400 feet a second) and had high trajectories (10 to 13½ inches midway for two hundred yards), but they were reliable, if proper elevation was given, up to three hundred to one thousand yards. Discriminating marksmen refused to use repeating rifles until they were made strong enough to handle ammunition of this or similar type.

The one fault of the long, heavy bullet was its high trajectory. It is hard to estimate distance correctly over uneven ground, across ravines, and over the water. It is harder still to make just the right allowance for it when aiming over open

SPORTING FIREARMS

sights. Moreover, game is hunted where there is cover. A man may not be expecting a shot at less than one hundred yards, but there is no telling when game may be jumped unexpectedly at some intermediate distance. Suppose he carries a .45-70, or a .38-55, sighted to strike center at one hundred yards. He jumps a deer at fifty yards, and fires quickly—no time to think about sight allowance. His rifle will shoot nearly three inches higher than he aims. This may mean all the difference between a clean kill and a cripple.

Had he been armed with a weapon taking such a cartridge as the 1906 model .30 U. S. A., the bullet would have risen no more than a negligible fraction of an inch above line of aim, at any point from muzzle to mark. At longer ranges than one hundred yards the advantage of a low trajectory rapidly mounts in value.

To meet the demand for a flatter line of fire in repeating rifles a new series of cartridges was devised, of which the .45-90-300 and .50-110-300 are typical. The total length of cartridge being limited by the form of breech mechanism, increased velocity could only be gained by enlarging the shell capacity and shortening the bullet.

Here, again, accuracy was sacrificed with no offsetting gain. The difference in trajectory be-

RIFLES AND AMMUNITION

tween the .45-90-300 and the .45-70-405 was so slight as to be of no practical value, considering that the latter bullet is the steadier of the two. Muzzle energies are the same, and the remaining energy of the 405 grain bullet is greater at all ranges than that of the 300. The .50-110-300, with a bullet of only one and one-third calibers length, and very blunt, is notoriously inaccurate, so that its trajectory figures are quite misleading. The .50-100-450, with longer bullet in the same shell is far superior to it in every respect.

Then came smokeless powder and steel-jacketed bullets, changing everything. We awoke to the fact that killing power or shock does not depend upon caliber alone. We also learned that a bullet

FIGURE 4.

of four or five calibers length could be given an initial speed of two thousand feet a second, or more, and yet shoot with precision at all ranges, with a trajectory lower even than that of the "sugar loaf" bullet from our grandfathers' muzzle-loader. The most effective sporting cartridges of this class are those using bullets of the length here mentioned, (*fig 4*), with lead exposed

SPORTING FIREARMS

at the tip so as to mushroom on impact. Weaker ammunition for medium game was provided in the .303 Savage, .30-30, .25-35, etc., with bullets of three to three and three-fourths calibers length, which were of fair accuracy and stopping power.

Some dissatisfaction has been found with ammunition for these small-bores, owing to defective bullets of the soft-point kind, which were not accurate and did not penetrate as they should. Consequently many hunters have insisted on larger calibers. An attempt to make high-velocity ammunition out of the old .45s and .50s was tried by returning again to the futile expedient of using bullets that were very short and stubby. It failed, as all such efforts are bound to fail, since a bullet that is inaccurate at moderate speed is sure to fly wilder and wilder as the velocity is increased. Other large caliber ammunition using longer bullets, such as the .35 Winchester, .405 Winchester, .9 mm. Mauser and Mannlicher, has given much better results.

Up to this point in the development of firearms, it seemed to have been proven that accuracy and sustained velocity could only be attained, in breech-loaders, by using long and heavy bullets. The lesson learned in muzzle-loading days that a great deal depends upon the shape of a projectile's

RIFLES AND AMMUNITION

head—upon its lines, as one would say of a boat—had been forgotten. Our riflemen and our gunmakers, as a class, seemed possessed of the notion that they had nothing to learn of their forefathers and nothing to learn abroad.

Meantime the U. S. A. ordnance board was getting interesting news from beyond the horizon. Smokeless powder and jacketed bullets were introduced from Europe; then came, from the same source, bolt action repeaters, clip-loading magazines, rimless shells, machines for charging cartridges by weight instead of by bulk, and, finally, an odd form of projectile, the sharp-pointed Spitzer bullet, which upset our so-called science of ballistics and taught us anew the lesson of the "sugar loaf."

The shape of the Spitzer bullet is shown in *fig. 5*, which is a view, partly in cross-section, of the

FIGURE 5.

.30 U. S. A. cartridge, model of 1906. The projectile is shorter than the former service bullet by about one-half caliber. Considerably more than

SPORTING FIREARMS

half its length forward is finely tapered from point to shoulder. In fact, only so much of the bullet is cylindrical as is necessary to give it secure bearing in the shell and a straight start in the bore of the gun.

Although the Spitzer weighs only one hundred and fifty grains, as against the two hundred and twenty of the old service bullet, its fine lines enable it to pierce the air much more easily than the old model with round head. When a bullet of the old form is made short enough to weigh only one hundred and fifty grains, and is fired with the same muzzle velocity as the sharp bullet, its speed falls off much more rapidly, and its trajectory is higher and higher as the range increases, until, at seven hundred yards, it even rises above that of the two hundred and twenty grain rounded-head bullet.

Form of bullet head becomes of greater and greater consequence as muzzle velocity is increased. It is much the same with projectiles in air as it is with boats in water—the higher the speed, the finer should be the lines. An ideal shape for a projectile would be somewhat like that of a submarine torpedo, sharp at both ends, and I doubt not that some day we shall come to it. In fact, I experimented with such missiles about

RIFLES AND AMMUNITION

twenty years ago and found that no sabot was needed to start them straight and that they required a much slower twist than bullets with square bases, which have to be shot light end foremost, in defiance of nature.

The change wrought by the Spitzer bullet has been as revolutionary, in its way, as that effected by smokeless powder. The maximum ordinate (highest rise) of the two hundred and twenty grain Springfield bullet, for one thousand yards range, is twenty-two feet; that for the sharp-point bullet is only fourteen and one-half feet. At all ranges up to two thousand yards the velocity of the sharp-point is greater and the trajectory flatter. Up to one thousand yards the energy is greater and the accuracy is better. In fact, the .30 U. S. A. cartridges turned out by the Frankford Arsenal since 1909 are probably the most accurate ammunition ever produced for a hand firearm, the mean radius at five hundred yards being 4.87 inches, and the mean vertical deviation 2.34 inches. When the rifle is sighted to strike center at one hundred and fifty yards, its bullet rises only 0.61 inch above actual line of sight at fifty yards, 1.05 inch at seventy-five yards, 1.07 inch at one hundred yards, 0.71 inch at one hundred and twenty-five yards, and falls only 1.19

SPORTING FIREARMS

inches below it at one hundred and seventy-five yards (my own figures).

Most surprising of all properties of this remarkable projectile is the fact, now well established, that the full-mantled bullet (not soft-nose) has tremendous smashing effect on living tissue and bones up to three hundred yards—quite enough for any American game.

I have written this sketch for a practical purpose. Since it is the cartridge that determines the kind of work that a rifle can do, it follows that when one is buying a rifle he first should consider the kind of work that he wants to do with it, then choose a cartridge adapted to such work. When this is settled, but not until then, it is time to consider what functioning mechanism is best for the purpose, what weight and proportions of arm, what materials and finish; then, finally, who makes the best gun of that kind. The trouble is that there are so many varieties of ammunition on our market that anyone studying catalogues and ballistic tables is likely to get " bumfuzzled," as my backwoods partner puts it. In the catalogue of one maker alone you can count more than four hundred different rifle cartridges, all of them on sale to-day. Nine out of ten of them are out-of-date, or of bad design. To criticize all of them

RIFLES AND AMMUNITION

would take a book. I have tried to show how one can discriminate by following a few safe rules:—

1. No cartridge is worthy of consideration by up-to-date sportsmen unless the bullet is at least—

```
3     calibers long for .25        caliber bullets
2½       "       "    "  .30 to .35   "      "
2        "                .40 to .45
1¾       "                .50
```

2. No bullet is accurate at high speed unless it either is long and heavy or has fine lines forward.

CHAPTER II

THE FLIGHT OF BULLETS

THE trajectory of a bullet is the curved path of its flight. Every missile travels in a constantly increasing curve. The height of that curve, for a given range, depends upon the speed at which the projectile flies. No trajectory can be flat, because no curve is flat; it will be low with a swift bullet and high with a slow one. The advantage of a low trajectory is that it extends the range throughout which one can hit game without making a close guess at the distance and precise allowance for the drop of bullet.

Imagine yourself hunting with an accurate but low-speed rifle—say a .38-55 or a .45-70 of the type favored a few years ago. In your hunting ground the cover is so thick that the guides say: "Don't bother about trajectory; nine-tenths of big game is shot within a hundred yards, and any rifle will carry 'level' enough to do the trick at that distance."

THE FLIGHT OF BULLETS

But the days slip by, your vacation is near spent, and you have no trophy. Then the extraordinary happens. A fine bull moose steps out to the lake's margin. There he stands, clearly outlined against sky and water, as fair a mark as any bull'seye on your target range at home. It is your last chance to retrieve from failure a trip you have planned these three years past, and one that has cost you a pretty penny, withal.

The beast is a good way off; just how far is not easy for city-trained eyes to gauge. You say to yourself " three hundred yards," and raise the rear sight accordingly. Beside you is a big, old mossy log—as good a muzzle rest as man could wish. It is a fair advantage to take for so long a shot. The moose does not wind you. There is no hurry. You aim as you never aimed before, draw trigger with never a blink or shrink, and—miss!

" Chr-r-ristopher Columbus! " or words to that effect.

The moose has vanished forever. And what's to blame? Trajectory is to blame. Your guide was right about the nine times in ten; but about this supreme and never-to-be-forgotten one chance in ten he was dead, dead wrong.

You overestimated the distance by fifty yards—not a very bad guess, under the circumstances. At

SPORTING FIREARMS

two hundred and fifty yards where the moose really stood, your slow-moving bullet, aimed for three hundred, flew nearly or quite two feet too high. Had you been armed with an accurate high-speed rifle, say a .30 U. S., '06, the bullet would have landed on the moose, from two to seven inches above the point you aimed at, with strong probability of bringing meat to camp and a fine head for the wall of your den at home.

These figures are not the kind reprinted by catalogue experts in the gun-talk pages of magazines. They are the kind that bring results. No gun ever shoots swift for one man and slow for another. Its trajectory is pre-determined when the cartridge is loaded, and one can no more alter it by anecdotes of fluke shots than he can by pulling harder on the trigger.

Trajectory, then, is something that every up-to-date sportsman should understand. To do so, one must give attention to a few figures. Those commonly printed in catalogue tables do not tell the facts that a hunter most needs to know. The midway rise of a bullet over certain ranges may have some value in comparing weapons, but little in hunting; for nobody will make a mistake of fifty per cent in judging distance. The zone of probable error is the twenty-five to seventy-five

THE FLIGHT OF BULLETS

yards nearest the mark shot at, both on the hither side and beyond the object.

Trajectory tables, to be of practical use to sportsmen, should show the height of bullet curve every twenty-five or fifty yards from muzzle to range sighted for; also the drop below line of aim, at similar intervals, for some distance beyond that range. It is not expedient to publish many such tables in this place, nor is it needful to do so. Rifle ammunition may be classified in a few well-defined groups, and a typical cartridge of each group will serve for comparison. The meaning of the tables published herewith can be taken in at a glance.

I have selected four typical cartridges, and give their trajectories, at sporting ranges, in detail. They may be compared with others by noting, first, the relative length of bullet in calibers, and, second, the midway height of curve over a given range, as shown in catalogues. The cartridges chosen for illustration are as follows—

(A). The .22 long rifle. Typical of miniature rim-fires used on very small game and vermin; also by beginners, as primers of marksmanship, and by older sportsmen to " keep their hands in."

(B). The .32 Winchester auto-loading cartridge. Type of cheap, short-range ammunition

SPORTING FIREARMS

suitable for shooting in settled regions at small game generally and at predatory creatures, yet powerful enough for an occasional deer or black bear.

(C). The well known .30-30. Differing but little from others in a series of cartridges of about two thousand feet a second muzzle velocity which are much used on game from deer to elk, having fairly low trajectory, fair accuracy, and enough power for all but the largest American game.

(D). The .30 U. S., model of 1906, with Spitzer bullet. Typical of the latest military and big game cartridges of highest velocity associated with fine accuracy and great shocking power.

The calculations are my own, checked against results of careful tests, and are close enough averages for all practical purposes. Be it remembered, however, that trajectories for the same arm vary a little, even at moderate ranges, according to atmospheric conditions and elevation above sea-level; more still, according to the vertical deviation of shots fired and the flip or stiffness of gun barrel. Some of these points will be considered later.

Trajectory is of practical interest to hunters in several ways:—

(1). It shows the extreme range to which a

THE FLIGHT OF BULLETS

given rifle can be sighted without letting the bullet rise more than a negligible amount above the line of aim; also the farthest range throughout which, without allowing for distance, it will neither rise above nor fall below a given animal's vitals when aimed at their center.

For example: I am hunting squirrels with a .22 taking the long-rifle cartridge. Squirrel range may be anywhere from fifteen to fifty yards. I adjust the rear sight, by targeting, to hit a nail head at thirty-five yards. The bullet's curve then will be as follows:—

(TABLE I.)

35 YARD TRAJECTORY OF .22 LONG-RIFLE.

Muzzle velocity 1,100 feet a second. Top of front sight ½ inch above axis of bore.

Trajectory, inches.	Distance, yards.							
	10	20	25	30	35	40	50	60
Above or below horizontal	0.39	0.47	0.40	0.25	0	—0.29	—1.30	—2.61
Sight allowance	.35	.21	.14	.07	0	.07	.21	.35
Above or below line of aim	0.04	0.26	0.26	0.18	0	—0.22	—1.09	—2.26

The *minus* sign indicates drop below line of sight.

SPORTING FIREARMS

Trajectories must be figured from the horizontal plane, which is a straight line from center of muzzle to the point the rear sight is adjusted for. But the curve that counts in hunting is that above or below line of aim, which is a straight line from top of front sight to the same point. The amount of sight allowance depends upon height of front sight (axis of a telescope sight) and is proportional to the distance.

In this instance my .22 bullet, starting half an inch below line of aim, cuts upward through that line at ten yards from the muzzle, rises to a quarter-inch above it, then falls to line of aim at thirty-five yards. If I shoot forty yards with the same sighting, I must aim a quarter of an inch high, to allow for drop; at fifty yards, one inch high; at sixty yards, two and one-quarter inches high.

Can I improve matters by adjusting for a fifty yard " point-blank? " Let me see:—

(TABLE II.)

50 YARD TRAJECTORY OF .22 LONG-RIFLE.

Trajectory, inches.	Distance, yards.							
	10	20	25	30	40	50	60	75
Above or below horizontal	0.65	0.99	1.05	1.03	0.75	0	—1.05	—3.26
Sight allowance	.42	.33	.25	.17	.08	0	.08	.25
Above or below line of aim	0.23	0.66	0.80	0.86	0.67	0	—0.97	—3.01

THE FLIGHT OF BULLETS

This curve is too high for squirrel shooting. The thirty-five yard point-blank was just right. For large animals, harder to approach, fifty yards might be the minimum.

(2). Such a trajectory table shows what allowance to make for drop of bullet beyond the point to which the sights are set. In making a quick shot beyond point-blank, one does not raise the rear sight. Either he draws a coarse bead, or he aims as much higher as he thinks the bullet will drop. The latter practice is best, for there is less guesswork about it.

(3. A set of trajectory tables for a certain cartridge, worked out for various ranges, shows how far it would be profitable to shoot at game of a given size with that charge—how far the bullet's curve will be low enough to give a reasonable chance of hitting. For instance: the .22 long-rifle cartridge will put ten consecutive shots in a three inch bull'seye at one hundred yards, or into an eight-inch bull'seye at two hundred yards, when the air is still.

Does this mean that it is fit to use at such ranges in hunting? Target shooters sometimes forget that there are no sighting shots at game. The precision required in judging distance with .22 long-rifle sighted for one hundred and two hundred yards, respectively, is shown below:—

SPORTING FIREARMS.

(TABLE III.)
100 YARD TRAJECTORY OF .22 LONG-RIFLE.

Trajectory, inches.   Distance, yards.

	25	50	75	100	125	150
Above or below horizontal ..	3.30	4.49	3.48	0	— 6.38	—15.37
Sight allowance	.38	.25	.13	0	.13	.25
Above or below line of aim	2.92	4.24	3.35	0	— 6.25	—15.12

(TABLE IV.)
200 YARD TRAJECTORY OF .22 LONG-RIFLE.

Trajectory ins.   Distance, yards.

	25	50	75	100	150	175	200	225
Above or below horizontal	8.84	15.59	20.12	22.20	17.93	10.67	0	—13.56
Sight allowance ..	.44	.38	.31	.25	.13	.06	0	.06
Above or below line of aim ...	8.40	15.21	19.81	21.95	17.80	10.61	0	—13.50

Everyone now and then makes a hit with the .22 at such ranges, but who keeps tally of the misses? Flukes are no proof of good marksmanship. No rim-fire .22 has a trajectory enough flatter than the above to make any material diffcrence in shooting. Further comment is needless.

Let us examine the curves of some cartridges

THE FLIGHT OF BULLETS

that are fit for serious hunting. The heights are given in inches and fractional parts:—

(TABLE V.)

TRAJECTORIES OF .32 WINCHESTER SELF-LOADING CARTRIDGE.

Muzzle velocity 1,392 feet a second.

Height of curve at	Range sighted to, in yards.					
	50	75	100	150	200	300
25 yards	0.6	1.3	2.0	3.5	5.2	....
50 "	0	1.4	2.7	5.8	9.2	17.2
75 "	—2.0	0	2.1	6.7	11.8	....
100 "	—5.5	—2.8	0	6.2	13.0	28.8
125 "	.....	—7.2	—3.7	4.0	12.5	....
150 "	.....	—13.5	—9.3	0	10.1	34.0
175 "	.....	.....	—16.5	—5.6	6.2	....
200 "	.....	.....	—25.9	—13.5	0	31.7
225 "	.....	.....	.....	.....	—7.1	....
250 "	.....	.....	.....	.....	—18.1	21.0
350 "	.....	.....	.....	.....	.....	—29.5

(TABLE VI.)

TRAJECTORIES OF .30-30, SOFT-NOSE 170 GRAIN BULLET.

Muzzle velocity 2,008 feet a second.

Height of curve at	Range sighted to, in yards.				
	75	100	150	200	300
25 yards	0.6	0.9	1.6	2.4	....
50 "	0.6	1.2	2.6	4.2	7.7
75 "	0	1.0	3.0	5.4	....
100 "	—1.3	0	2.8	5.9	12.9
125 "	—3.3	—1.7	1.8	5.6	....
150 "	—6.1	—4.2	0	4.6	15.2
175 "	.....	—7.5	—2.6	2.8	....
200 "	.....	—11.7	—6.2	0	14.2
225 "	.....	.....	—10.7	—3.7	....
250 "	.....	.....	—16.2	—8.5	19.2
300 "	.....	.....	.....	—21.2	0
350 "	.....	.....	.....	.....	—14.7
400 "	.....	.....	.....	.....	—35.8

SPORTING FIREARMS

(TABLE VII.)

TRAJECTORIES OF .30 U. S., MODEL OF 1906.

Muzzle velocity 2,700 feet a second.

Height of curve at	Range sighted to, in yards.				
	150	200	300	400	500
25 yards...........	0.8	1.2	2.0	.....	....
50 "	1.3	2.0	3.6	5.4	7.6
75 "	1.6	2.6	5.0	.....	....
100 "	1.4	2.9	6.1	9.8	14.1
125 "	0.9	2.7	6.3	.....	....
150 "	0	2.3	7.1	12.7	19.1
175 "	—1.4	1.3	6.8	.....	....
200 "	—3.1	0	6.5	14.0	22.4
225 "	—5.3	—1.8	6.2	.....	....
250 "	—7.9	—4.1	4.6	13.6	24.3
275 "	......	—6.8	2.7	.....	....
300 "	......	—10.0	0	11.2	24.1
350 "	......	......	—5.7	8.0	22.4
400 "	......	......	—14.7	0	17.1
450 "	......	......	......	—10.0	9.3
500 "	......	......	......	—21.5	0
550 "	......	......	......	......	—11.4

(TABLE VIII.)

150 YARD TRAJECTORY OF .30 U. S., WITH SIGHT ALLOWANCE.

Top of front sight one inch above axis of bore.

Trajectory ins.	Distance, yards.							
	25	50	75	100	125	150	175	200
Above or below horizontal.	0.83	1.28	1.55	1.40	0.88	0	—1.36	—3.01
Sight allowance ..	.84	.67	.50	.33	.17	0	.17	.33
Above or below line of aim ...	—0.01	0.61	1.05	1.07	0.71	0	—1.19	—2.68

The mean vertical deviation of the .30 U. S.,

THE FLIGHT OF BULLETS

'06, service cartridge should be added, proportionally, to the trajectories, in order to get the average height of shots that fly high, and subtracted for the average of those that go low, for no two shots from the same gun describe exactly the same curve.

This is a matter of importance, yet it is seldom taken into account. Trajectory figures are trustworthy, *provided the gun and cartridge are steady performers*; otherwise they are not. It is of little use to know the average curve of a series of fliers and drop-shots.

In the *Forest and Stream* trajectory test of 1885, a .50-95-300 rifle showed an average trajectory of 1.178 inches midway over the one hundred yard range. This was the mean height of five consecutive shots, fired from machine rest, through a paper screen at fifty yards. A .40-70-330 rifle, tested in the same way, gave an average rise of 2.452 inches at the same distance. If those averages alone had been published, most readers would have concluded that the curve of the .50 was much the best. But the shot-for-shot records showed that the .50-95 actually varied 4.29 inches vertically in those five test shots at fifty yards, whereas the .40-70 varied only 0.17 inch in its five shots.

This is an extreme instance; still, the difference

SPORTING FIREARMS

in vertical deviation between popular cartridges of to-day is too great to be overlooked in this connection. Some will put a long series of shots into a four-inch bull'seye at two hundred yards; others will often miss a twelve-inch one.

Lieutenant Townsend Whelen, U. S. A., one of our highest authorities on modern rifles, has shown that the .30 Krag cartridge (commonly known as the .30-40), and others of the two thousand foot class, when charged with soft-nose bullets for hunting, will not make a sure hit at more than half the range that a .30 U. S. sharp-point will, the arm in each case being sighted to its farthest effective " point-blank " for deer, no allowance for distance being made in aiming. He adds to the trajectory of each cartridge its mean vertical deviation over the range sighted for, and this is the only fair comparison.

I quite agree with him that accuracy and trajectory must be considered together, not separately, and that makers of guns and ammunition should publish the mean radius of shots fired from machine rest, as well as the trajectory curve, for each cartridge, at various sporting ranges. It is by no means satisfactory to say " accurate to (so many) yards," or " accurate enough for hunting purposes." The buyer is the man to define what

THE FLIGHT OF BULLETS

"accurate" means, and he should have definite measurements to compare by.

If a gun adds to a man's error of holding a quite appreciable error of its own, it is fit for nothing but the scrap heap. If high velocity could only be attained by sacrificing precision of fire, it would not be worth having. It is entirely practicable nowadays to make rifles and ammunition (of any caliber and any reasonable power) so accurate that they will shoot as close as a good marksman can hold, under favorable field conditions. No lower standard than this should be accepted for any rifle.

CHAPTER III

KILLING POWER

THE all-round effectiveness of a bullet depends upon its penetration and the shock it imparts. Penetration is determined chiefly by the length of bullet in calibers and its resistance to deformation. Other things being equal, the longer the bullet the deeper it will pierce. Shock depends upon energy spent in the blow and upon area and nature of wound.

In comparing the killing power of different charges we have one definite datum to start with: the muzzle energy of the bullet. Energy is expressed in foot-pounds, which means the force required to lift so many pounds one foot from the ground. Energy varies directly as the bullet's weight and as the square of its velocity. Speed, then, is of greater consequence than weight of bullet. For example:

Weight of bullet.	Muzzle velocity.	Muzzle energy.
150 grains.	1,500 feet a second.	750 foot-pounds.
300 grains.	1,500 feet a second.	1,499 foot-pounds.
150 grains.	3,000 feet a second.	2,998 foot-pounds.

KILLING POWER

In this instance, doubling the weight only doubles the energy; but doubling the speed quadruples the energy. Notice that caliber has nothing to do with this. Weight and velocity determine the resulting energy, no matter what the caliber may be.

But game is seldom shot at the muzzle of the gun. The energy we are interested in is energy at point of impact, wherever that may be. Bullets differ very much in the degree to which they maintain or lose speed and energy. The 200-grain bullet of a .401 self-loader (very short and bluff) loses thirty-five per cent of its energy in going only one hundred yards; the 300-grain .405 (medium length and taper) loses twenty-six per cent; the 150-grain .30 sharp-point U. S. bullet (relatively longer, and with fine taper) loses but sixteen and one-half per cent energy in the same distance. Here is another reason for observing critically the length of bullet in calibers (*i. e.*, length in proportion to diameter) when choosing a cartridge.

Let us now compare the muzzle energies of the leading hunting cartridges, this being the first step toward estimating their relative efficiency in hunting. I have selected fifty or more standard ones, ranging from the weakest to the most powerful that are used in magazine arms at the date of this

SPORTING FIREARMS

writing. Just now we are entering a new era of military and sporting firearms. Improved ammunition of American design will probably be on the market before long. Meantime, in order to be up-to-date, I must use a number of foreign ones for illustration of recent progress in ammunition for big game.

In classifying cartridges under the three heads of big game, medium game, and small game ammunition, I have drawn the dividing lines at two thousand and at seven hundred foot-pounds muzzle energy, respectively. Judging from results observed in the field, I think this rating is as fair as any arbitrary standard can be. Much, of course, depends upon local conditions and the method of hunting. The .25-35, for example, is an excellent little cartridge for all-round use in a country where turkeys or geese and small mammals are the commonest game, yet where deer and black bear are met now and then. If deer and bear were plentiful enough to be the main object of chase, one would prefer a cartridge of greater energy.

When a man is hunting sheep, goats, or elk, with possible grizzlies as a side issue, the .30 U. S. could be recommended without question. If he were making a specialty of grizzlies, or of the more formidable Alaskan or polar bears, he might do

KILLING POWER

well to accept the burden and kick of a .333 or a .425. The largest game on this continent has been killed by thousands with rifles using ammunition that I class as "medium game." I have known an Arkansas hunter who was credited with having killed over five hundred black bears in the brakes and cypress sloughs surrounding his own plantation, and he would scarcely touch any other rifle than the .32-20 Winchester model of 1873, which is here rated as for small game.

Three weeks ago, one of my hunting partners, while trout fishing, came upon a two-year-old bear in the thicket. He knocked it down by a lucky throw of a stone no bigger than a billiard ball, hitting the beast at butt of the ear, and finished it with his pocket knife. Some years earlier, another partner of mine, within a mile of this same place, shot a small bear in the head with a .44-40 and jumped into the scrimmage to kick his dogs loose. The bear was practically unhurt and turned on him. "Doc" conquered, but he came to me in a condition that he described as "nigh breechless." One can draw his own inferences about proper weapons for bears.

The ballistics of this or that cartridge vary somewhat according to the factory loading it. Where this variation is considerable, I give the

SPORTING FIREARMS

data supplied by different ammunition companies. The following abbreviations are used: *U. M. C.,* Union Metallic Cartridge Co.; *U. S.,* United States Cartridge Co.; *Win.,* Winchester Repeating Arms Co.; *B.,* blunt headed bullet (whether rounded or flat tipped); *S.,* sharp-point bullet. Ballistics of foreign cartridges are those of foreign, not domestic, loading. Length of bullet may be judged from its weight, as contrasted with others of the same caliber.

BIG GAME CARTRIDGES.

Caliber, inch.	Cartridge.	Bullet grains.		M.Vel. ft.secs.	M.En. ft.lbs.
.256 (6.5 mm.)	Mauser and Mannl	157	B.	2313	1960
.256 6.5 mm.)	Mauser and Mannl	139	S.	2887	2585
.256 (6.5 mm.)	Mannlicher-Schoenauer	123	S.	2592	1845
.278 (7 mm.)	Mauser and Mannl	173	B.	2231	2025
.278 (7 mm.)	Mauser and Mannl	154	S.	2740	2568
.278 (7 mm.)	Mauser and Mannl	139	S.	2920	2632
.280 Ross		140	S.	3150	3095
.280 Ross		160	S.	2950	3088
.30 Krag, '98 (.30-40)		220	B.	2005	1972
.30 Krag, Hudson-Thomas		202	S.	2160	2094
.30 U. S., '06, service		150	S.	2700	2429
.30 U. S., match		172	S.	2580	2540
.315 (8 mm.)	Mauser and Mannl	236	B.	2034	2221
.315 (8 mm.)	Mauser and Mannl	154	S.	2882	2823
.315 8 mm.)	Mannlicher-Schoenauer	244	B.	2165	2540
.315 (8 mm.)	Mannlicher-Schoenauer	170	S.	2411	2199
.333 Jeffery-Mauser		250	S.	2600	4200
.35 Win., model 1895		250	B.	2200	2687
.350 Rigby-Mauser		225	S.	2572	3306

KILLING POWER

.355 (9 mm.) Mannlicher	281 B.	2100	2700
.401 Win., self-loader	200 B.	2142	2038
.401 Win., self-loader	250 B.	1875	1952
.405 Win., model 1895	300 B.	2204	3237
.413 (10.5 mm.) Mannlicher	309 B.	2230	2935
.425 Westley Richards-Mauser	410 S.	2350	5022
.441 (11 mm.) Mauser	322 B.	2461	3969

MEDIUM GAME CARTRIDGES.

.22 High Power Savage	68 B.	2800	1200	
.25-35 Win. and Savage	117 B.	2030	1070	
.25-35 Rem., Stand., Stev	117 B.	2127	1175	
.25-35 Rem., Stand., self-loading	101 S.	2275	1158	
.25-36 Marlin	117 B.	1855	893	U.M.C.
.30-30 Win., Marl., Sav	170 B.	2008	1522	
.30-30 Rem., Stand., Stev	170 B.	2020	1540	
.30-30 Rem., Stand., self-loading	151 S.	2020	1450	
.303 Savage	195 B.	1952	1658	U.M.C.
.32-40 Win., Marl., Sav., H.V.	165 B.	2065	1558	U.M.C.
.32-40 Win., Marl., Sav., H.V.	165 B.	1752	1125	Win.
.32 Special Win. and Marl.	165 B.	2112	1684	
.32 Rem., Stand., Stev	165 B.	2057	1550	
.32 Win., self-loading	165 B.	1392	710	
.33 Win	200 B.	2056	1878	
.35 Rem., Stand., Stev	200 B.	2000	1776	
.35 Rem., Stand., self-loading	170 S.	2050	1585	
.35 Win., self-loading	180 B.	1396	779	
.351 Win., self-loading	180 B.	1861	1385	
.38-55 Win., Marl., Sav., H.V.	255 B.	1700	1635	U.M.C.
.38-55 Win., Marl., Sav., H.V.	255 B.	1593	1437	Win.
.40-65 Win. and Marl., H.V.	253 B.	1790	1800	

SMALL GAME CARTRIDGES.

.22 short, rim-fire	30 B.	900	54	U.M.C.
.22 short, rim-fire	30 B.	975	63	U.M.C.
.22 long, rim-fire	30 B.	1000	66	
.22 long-rifle and armory, rim-fire	40 B.	1100	108	
.22 long-rifle, smokeless, rim-fire	40 B.	983	86	

SPORTING FIREARMS

.22 automatic, rim-fire........	45 B.	1036	107 U.M.C.
.22 automatic, rim-fire........	45 B.	1000	100 U.S.
.22 automatic, rim-fire........	45 B.	903	82 Win.
.22-7 Win., rim fire model 1890..	45 B.	1150	132 U.S.
.22-7 Win., rim fire model 1890..	45 B.	1107	123 Win.
.22-7 Win., rim fire model 1890..	45 B.	1036	107 U.M.C.
.22-13-45 Win., center-fire.....	45 B.	1541	237
.25 Stevens, rim-fire..........	67 B.	1161	201
.25-20 Win., single-shot........	86 B.	1468	412
.25-20 Win., & Marl., repeater.	86 B.	1547	457 U.M.C.
.25-20 Win., & Marl., repeater.	86 B.	1376	362 Win.
.25-20 Win., & Marl., repeater, H. V...................	86 B.	1711	560
.32-20 Win., & Marl..........	100 B.	1325	390 U.M.C.
.32-20 Win., & Marl..........	115 B.	1222	382 Win.
.32-20 Win., & Marl., H. V....	100 B.	1575	551 U.M.C.
.32-20 Win., & Marl., H. V....	115 B.	1640	690 Win.

One material fact that shows conspicuously in these tables is that caliber alone is no gauge of power. Let the novice rid himself, once and for all, of the notion that a big bore necessarily means a powerful rifle and a small bore means a weak one. This never was true, even in the days of round bullets. As far back as the American Revolution our frontiersmen of the Alleghanies discovered and adopted the " express " system of driving small bullets at very high speed, thus getting the maximum efficiency out of a given weight of lead.

In our tables of modern ammunition we see a .35 caliber Winchester of 779 foot-pounds muzzle energy, and another .35 Winchester of 2,687 foot-pounds. The former is rather light for deer

KILLING POWER

shooting, and the latter will knock out a grizzly bear. Again, we note a bullet of only .256 inch diameter and 139 grains weight, that has a muzzle energy of 2,585 foot-pounds, which is much greater than that of any .45 or .50 caliber cartridge loaded with black gunpowder that ever was used in a repeating arm. It attains this power by a muzzle velocity of 2,887 feet a second.

We come, now, to a matter of caliber that does affect killing power. It is not the normal diameter of the bullet, but its diameter when expanded by impact. This latter factor determines, in great degree, how much of the projectile's energy will actually be *utilized* in shocking the thing struck. Here is where the question of big bores *vs.* small bores really hinges.

The pressure and heat of smokeless powder and the quick twist of rifling required by modern arms compel us to use bullets wholly or partly encased in jackets of hard metal. The fault of a full-jacketed bullet is that, unless driven at extremely high speed, it only punches a small hole through a beast, piercing so easily that it does not expend much of its energy on the object struck, but wastes it in flight beyond. Such a missile can pass close to a vital organ without disturbing it, close to a nerve without severely

SPORTING FIREARMS

shocking it, close to a blood vessel without rupturing it. The hole of exit is little if any larger than that of entrance, and both of them contract so as not to let out blood.

A good bullet for hunting any big game except the greater pachyderms is one that will expand when it hits, and still hold together so as to penetrate deeply. Such a bullet " pulps " tissue all around its course, drives body fluids violently away from it, smashes bones instead of drilling them, paralyzes nerves, and either imparts its full blow by stopping in the body or tears a big hole of exit through which the life-blood rapidly drains. This sounds gruesome, but in fact it is humane; for the quicker a beast is knocked down and dispatched, the better it is for all concerned.

To make a manteled bullet expand on impact, its tip must be so modified as to open and let part of the lead core flatten out. In a full-jacketed bullet the metal casing does not cover the butt end. If the tip, then, is split or filed across, there is risk of the lead core being blown forward and through it, stripping the jacket and perhaps lodging it in the gun barrel. If this happens, and is not discovered before the next shot, the barrel will either be bulged or burst. Special bullets are manufactured abroad that have the head split

KILLING POWER

back of the tip (*fig. 6*) leaving the latter intact.

Figure 6.

Their effectiveness depends upon so many contingencies that they are scarcely to be recommended.

Hollow bullets have been employed for many years. If driven to low speed the cavity must be deep (*fig. 7*) to insure expansion; if at higher speed, it must be shallower (*fig. 8*) or the missile

Figure 7.   Figure 8.

will spread prematurely and fly to fragments, making only a superficial wound. For cartridges of great velocity the hollow must be shallow (*fig. 9*) and backed by a long core of lead. In such

Figure 9.

case a plug, wedge, or steel ball (Hoxie bullet)

SPORTING FIREARMS

may be fitted into the mouth of the cavity to compel the tip to spread when its hits.

In general it may be said of hollow bullets that they are ill-balanced and therefore inaccurate at any but short range. Their action is uncertain, because velocity depends upon range, animals vary a great deal in toughness of hide and tissue, and a hollow bullet that would merely flatten on flesh or viscera might fly to flinders on bone.

Up to date, the favorite expanding bullet in our country is what is called the "soft-nose" (*figs. 10, 12*). This is solid throughout, but

FIGURE 10.

FIGURE 12.

has the base covered by the hard metal envelope and the tip left with more or less of the lead core exposed. A well proportioned and well made bullet of this sort generally gives satisfaction. Its expansion depends upon how much lead is left naked at the tip, this being regulated according to the velocity of impact. It will not do to expose too much of it, nor to make the tip flat, because such a ball is easily deformed and is prone to jam when fed upward at a slant from the maga-

KILLING POWER

zine; neither will it fly accurately, nor with normal speed.

A short soft-nose bullet (*fig. 10*) is not so reliable as a long one (*fig. 12*), because it upsets throughout so much of its length (*fig. 11*) that it

FIGURE 11.

is prone to go to pieces, especially on bone, and fail to pierce deep enough. A long bullet mushrooms at the tip only (*fig. 13*) and has a solid

FIGURE 13.

cylinder back of it to drive ahead. Thickness of jacket modifies such action a good deal; also softness or hardness of the leaden core.

Any soft-nose bullet should have its length, strength of mantel, and temper and relative exposure of tip carefully proportioned to the power of the gun and the character of game hunted; otherwise it will not give satisfaction. Soft-nose

SPORTING FIREARMS

bullets of Spitzer shape, to be propelled at very high speed, have but little of the point left naked (*fig. 14*). They are more likely to be accurate fliers than round-headed ones.

FIGURE 14.

The fact that the base of a soft-nose is covered by the metal envelope affects its upsettage on firing. Hence it may be advisable to make such bullets a trifle super-caliber, to insure that they seal the bore gas-tight when they issue from the cartridge shell. Lack of care in this respect accounts, I think, for much of the inaccuracy that has been observed with bullets of this class.

Recently a capped bullet has been introduced (*fig. 15*) consisting of a cylindrical core of lead

FIGURE 15.

encased in hard metal, dished out in front like the "man-stopper" revolver bullet, and covered at the head with a hollow cap of thin copper. It expands with certainty, yet holds together and

KILLING POWER

penetrates well, inflicting a very severe wound. In Spitzer bullets the cap is pointed and the front of core has a shallow cavity (*fig. 16*).

FIGURE 16.

Until further reports are received from the field, covering all kinds of big game hunting, it is too early to determine whether the expanding principle should or should not be applied to Spitzer bullets for general hunting. The sharp-point bullet, with its high velocity, has revolutionized military ammunition and is likely to do the same for sporting arms of all calibers. When used in proper barrels it is the most accurate missile known. It maintains speed and energy so much better than those with rounded or ogival head that ballistic tables employed in the old way will not serve to calculate its curve of flight, which is much lower than that of an old-style projectile of the same caliber, same weight, and same muzzle velocity.

More extraordinary still is the fact that instead of the sharp-point penetrating bone or tissue more easily and with less disruption of channel, as we naturally would expect, it will, when striking at

SPORTING FIREARMS

very high speed, smash and pulp a considerable area around the bullet's course, thereby delivering a paralyzing, knock-out blow. It is the full-jacketed Spitzer of which I speak—the regular military pattern.

At the extreme speed of close quarters it is checked or stopped by less thickness of flesh or bone than at long range. If it goes through, the wound of exit is large and lacerated. All this depends upon very high velocity, the minimum required for knock-out effect seeming to be about 2,000 feet a second at point of impact (not muzzle of gun) which corresponds to a range of 300 yards with the .30 Springfield-Mauser* used by our army and navy. At low speed the Spitzer merely drills a small hole, like that of the older military bullet.

To sum up: energy actually utilized in shock depends upon resistance offered by the animal's body. Resistance, so far as the missile is concerned, depends upon (1) the size to which the bullet mushrooms, or (2) upon the speed of bullet being so high that tissues and body fluids cannot give way easily to let the projectile pass, but

---

* I call our service arm the Springfield-Mauser because it is a Mauser action slightly modified by our ordnance board. A second-hand gun of another kind has recently been marketed under the trade name of "Springfield-Mauser," which will not take our service ammunition and is inferior in every respect.

KILLING POWER

set up a sudden and violent pressure all around the neighborhood of the wound, with consequent shattering effect over a large area.

A large bullet is more effective than a small one *provided* that its velocity is correspondingly great and that it is not too short to maintain energy and hold together so as to penetrate. The minimum length permissible, in calibers, that I mentioned in Chapter I, is a good rule-of-thumb by which to judge force as well as accuracy. In case of doubt, use a still longer bullet. Short bullets are not fit to use on any but soft-skinned game, and then only at short range. To trust them on dangerous beasts is folly.

American riflemen of the old school inclined toward very light charges. There was a time when game was so plentiful and (relatively) so unwary that a hunter generally had a fair chance to display exquisite marksmanship—the art of the nail-driver—at the short ranges that were then the rule.

Conditions change. We take running shots nowadays and long shots that our forefathers would have considered foolish. In such hunting it is utterly impossible to "put the bullet in the right place" so unfailingly as of yore. To be humane, then—to be sportsmen instead of butchers

SPORTING FIREARMS

and bunglers—we must use charges of much greater power than were customary a quarter of a century ago. This we still can do with small bores, owing to improved ammunition.

The advantages of a small bore are plain: a light and handy weapon, comfortable in the saddle or on an all-day tramp, light ammunition, moderate recoil, low trajectory, fine accuracy, and efficiency to the farthest sporting ranges.

Having spoken at length of big game ammunition, I may add a few words on the much simpler matter of cartridges for small game.

The .22 short, of good make, is very accurate up to thirty-five yards, but unreliable beyond fifty. Its proper use is for miniature target practice and exterminating vermin. To employ so feeble a charge on squirrels, rabbits, or game birds is cruel, because many will escape in crippled condition. The .22 long is not so accurate and has no superior merit of any kind, the difference in trajectory and killing power between it and the .22 short being microscopic.

The .22 long-rifle is the most accurate rim-fire cartridge of its caliber. Varieties of it called armory cartridges, and known as the .22 Krag, .22 U. S., and .22 Stevens-Pope, differ only in having the bullet firmly seated in the shell so as not

KILLING POWER

to pull out in the barrel throat when a loaded cartridge is ejected—a distinct advantage. The .22 automatic is of variable merit, as will be seen in the table. The best rim-fire hunting cartridge of this caliber is the .22-7 Winchester, model of 1890. It is accurate to one hundred and fifty yards and has considerably greater killing power than either of the others; in fact it is the only .22 rim-fire that should be used on game larger than squirrels.

For turkeys, geese, and the lesser animals, nothing under a .25 caliber should be used, unless it be the .22-15-60 Stevens, which is limited to single-loaders, or the new .22 high power. The .25-20 is a standard charge for such game when hunted near settlements.

A much better cartridge, wherever it can safely be used, is the .25-35. This is the most accurate medium power charge of the 2,000 foot-second class that we have at present and gives but half the recoil of a .30-30. It is far more reliable in windy weather than a .25-20. With a telescope sight on the rifle, sharpshooting at geese and other wary game can be practiced with deadly effect at two hundred yards, or even farther.

The .22 high-power cartridge, recently introduced, has not been standarized at the time of this

SPORTING FIREARMS

writing. Its ballistics, as given in my table, are subject to modification. It is a striking example of the killing power of a very small, solid, sharp-point bullet, when driven at great speed. Although the missile weighs only 68 grains, it is more destructive than the 180-grain bullet of a .35 Winchester self-loader; and it is also more accurate.

CHAPTER IV

RIFLE MECHANISMS AND MATERIALS

THE typical sporting rifle of to-day is a repeating arm. Repeaters are classified according to form of magazine and system of breech mechanism.

A tubular magazine under the barrel has several defects and no compensating merits. It is needlessly cumbersome and complicated, easily injured, awkward to recharge, prone to make a rifle jam in feeding. The position of the cartridge, end to end, is unsafe in principle. Soft-nose bullets are battered or scraped, and sharp-points cannot be used at all, in a tubular magazine. The balance and symmetry of the gun are spoiled.

A box magazine, with cartridges superimposed, has none of these faults. But if it protrudes much in front of the trigger guard it is unsightly and always in the way. Since it sticks out at the very point where a gun should balance, it will be a wearying annoyance on every all-day trip.

A revolving magazine inside the receiver is a

SPORTING FIREARMS

further improvement. It is somewhat bothersome to recharge, hard to unload, and occasionally may balk in feeding.

Decidedly the best magazine is a flat one within the receiver, flush with the forearm, carrying cartridges in double column, and charged either by clips or by dropping the cartridges in and settling them to place by one or two slight motions of a finger lever.

Whatever the system of magazine, there should be a cut-off whereby the arm can be used as a single-loader, so that special ammunition may be used when desired, with a magazine full of regular cartridges in reserve.

As regards method of operating, magazine rifles are either trombone action, lever action, bolt action or self-loading arms.

The trombone action with sliding forearm ("pump gun") can be fired faster, with good aim, than any other repeater that is operated by hand. It is the only system, except the self-loader, that can compete with a double barrel in getting in a quick and sure second shot. In rifles it is the best hand-functioned mechanism for small cartridges. For heavy charges it is not reliable, since it has not enough power to feed and extract refractory cartridges. It is too frail for weapons

MECHANISMS AND MATERIALS

that are to be taken into rough service in remote regions.

Lever actions vary a good deal in merit. As a class, they are quite satisfactory for ammunition of medium power, and in arms that are to be used only on short and easy trips. If the bolt is closed by double locking bolts near head of cartridge, as in the '86 model Winchester, the action will withstand any strain that a barrel can stand. If, however, there is but one locking bolt, and it in the rear, there will be a certain spring or play of the bolt proper which affects accuracy. It is unreliable in case of a defective high-power cartridge or an unnoticed obstruction in the barrel. In some actions of this character the lever, being held only friction-tight, soon wears shackly and sags in a most annoying way.

Both lever and trombone actions are prone to jam, especially if the rifle be uptilted in reloading, as when one lowers his rifle from the shoulder while working the lever or slide. Such balks generally occur at the worst possible moment. I have had this happen with a brand new weapon at the second shot. While I was prying at the cartridge a deer actually stopped as if to hear what I had to say about the matter. Then it took genuine alarm.

SPORTING FIREARMS

Nearly all rifles that operate by lever or trombone slide are complicated, hard to take apart for cleaning or repair, and hard to reassemble. There is a multitude of small parts that are likely to roll away and be lost while you are struggling to fit things together. You must have two or three screwdrivers and a pin punch to work with. The job will take from half an hour to half a day, depending upon whether you happen to have printed instructions to go by or only the light of nature and average awkwardness. Of course, if your hunting range is near home, accidents will be few and the gunsmith handy; but if you are forty miles from Nowhere, with a gun that has dropped in the mud, or in the water, or has got sanded, or has snapped off a spring, or broken a firing-pin, and you have no tool to work with but the file you sharpen your axe with—then is the time that good little deer should not stop to listen.

No lever or trombone action can be cleaned from the breech (the only way that a good rifle should be cleaned) unless it has a detachable barrel. The common pattern of take-down works by an interrupted screw at the breech. The barrel thereby is weakened at the very point where it should be strongest. Such a mechanism will

MECHANISMS AND MATERIALS

soon wear shaky. I have yet to see a take-down action that is trustworthy for big game rifles.

In this connection it may be remarked that everybody hates to clean a gun when he comes in at night, fagged out from a hard day's chase. The easier the gun is to clean, the likelier it is to be cleaned. And a night or two of neglect may ruin the finest rifle in the world.

It is significant that no lever or trombone action has ever passed a modern ordnance board or been adopted by any civilized army. While the requirements of rifles for small game and target practice are less stringent than for those built for military service, there is no difference at all between those of big game rifles and military ones, as regards strength, simplicity, ease of dismounting, and certainty of working properly in any emergency. There was a time when ordnance boards were conservative to a fault, and when private manufacturers took the lead in improving firearms, but that time has past. The sportsman of to-day who goes far into wild regions, and who must depend upon his rifle at times to preserve his life, should give close heed to the latest and best in military weapons, for the highest technical skill in the world is engaged on that class of firearms.

SPORTING FIREARMS

Bolt action repeaters of the best military or semi-military type are simple, strong, durable, and sure to function. In such a weapon the bolt can be slipped out in a second, so that the barrel can be inspected and cleaned from the breech. The entire working mechanism can be taken apart with the fingers, or, at most, with a single screwdriver or key. There are but few parts, and all of them amply strong. Coiled springs, practically unbreakable, take the place of flat springs that always are treacherous.

A bolt action locks with two lugs immediately behind the cartridge head, and there is a third, or even a fourth, lug in the rear. Such closure will withstand the breech pressure of any cartridge. The extractor is equal to any strain. Since the extractor engages the head of the shell before feeding into the chamber, a refractory cartridge can be ejected instantly instead of having to be pried out. A bolt action works better than any other when the arm has become foul from grit, as is bound to occur at times in sandy countries. Finally, all bolt actions of recent model have flush magazines, easy to recharge, and the best of them are supplied with cut-offs.

The only objection urged against bolt actions is that they are awkward to manipulate and slow

MECHANISMS AND MATERIALS

in repeating. This is largely a matter of habit. A man shoots best with the action he is used to. Anyone who watches soldiers in their skirmish runs and rapid fire practice can see that the common military bolt can be worked fast enough for almost any emergency that may happen in hunting. For the extremely rapid work sometimes needed in the close quarters of thicket or jungle shooting, where a rifle is not aimed but pointed, as one would point a shotgun or a revolver. a self-loader ranks first, with the straight-pull bolt a close second, the lever action third, and the bolt of four motions a lagging fourth. Here, however, we should consider that a quick first shot of great smashing power is generally worth more than three or four hits rained with ammunition of low or medium power; that very quick repeating is almost never done with any but weak ammunition; and that the bolt action handles powerful charges better than any other repeater.

In my opinion, the only speed of fire, with rifles that is worth considering is speed of *aimed* fire. No kind of gun can deliver a second shot accurately until both it and its user have recovered equilibrium. The time required to catch fresh aim will depend upon how hard the gun recoils. With weak ammunition that gives practically no

SPORTING FIREARMS

recoil, the only disturbance to be corrected is that caused by operating the gun's mechanism. When powerful charges are used in aimed fire, the straight-pull bolt is quickest, and between the lever and the turn-down bolt there is little difference.

This brings us naturally to the topic of self-loading arms. It is claimed that they " absorb " much of the recoil. With present-day patterns I do not find it so. The shock is more of a push than a kick, but it disturbs aim just as much, with cartridge of given power. So long as a self-loader is used only with weak ammunition it can be fired a little faster, with good aim, than any other mechanism; but it is not yet made to handle really first-class ammunition for big game or military purposes. I do not regard the extra quickness of the self-loader as of so much value as another merit that seldom is considered, namely: its noiselessness in recharging. If one's first shot misses, the animal is likely to pause for an instant, listening and scenting to get the direction of danger. Then the *clank—clank* of a hand-operated arm tells just what the beast wants to know: whereupon it is off on the jump, and you have lost the chance of a standing shot.

MECHANISMS AND MATERIALS

The objections that have been made against lever and trombone actions apply with yet greater force to self-loaders as we know them to-day. Glancing backward over the history of firearms, one will observe that from muzzle-loaders to breech-loaders, from single-shot arms to magazine guns, from hand-operated repeaters to our so-called automatics, every gain in rapidity of fire has been made, at first, by sacrificing the more essential merits of simplicity, reliability, and power.

Our self-loading rifles just now are in this experimental stage. They are good enough for light work in the neighborhood of settlements, or as auxiliaries when one has a ship or a caravan to fall back on; but as weapons for hard service they do not compare with a first-class bolt action rifle using the best type of ammunition for big game. None the less, we all expect the "automatic" to win in the end; and few of us would be surprised to learn to-morrow that the thing was done.

I repeat that the faults of lever and trombone actions, self-loaders, and this or that style of magazine, are not of serious consequence so long as the guns are used with ammunition of moderate power and in regions where repairs can easily be

SPORTING FIREARMS

made. Mechanically, and from a strictly impartial standpoint, the bolt action is the highest development of rifle construction at the time of this writing. Lever and trombone are out-of-date for all but light work, and auto-loaders are ahead of the times. But mechanical perfection is not the only point to be noted in a general review of present-day arms. Most of our people still prefer the older models, partly because we are used to them, and partly because they happen to be cheaper.

Here we should consider that the rifle trade in America is on a different basis from that of any other manufacturing country. In no other civilized nation are sporting firearms so generally owned and used by all classes of people. Probably nine male Americans out of ten, of military age, own guns of one sort or another. New rifles, shotguns, and revolvers or pistols, are sold by the myriad every year. It follows, as a matter of course, that the chief demand here is for " a cheap gun that will do the work." And it follows, as a matter of business, that our home gunmakers turn out the best cheap guns in the world. They also make, for those who will pay the price, as good shotguns as can be found anywhere, and revolvers that are simply peerless.

MECHANISMS AND MATERIALS

We cannot say the same for our rifles. The demand for really first-class rifles has not yet reached the proportions that justify large expenditures to produce them. It is growing so rapidly, however, that one may expect decided improvements within the next ten years. Among our better informed sportsmen it already is insistent. Many of them purchase foreign weapons. Others take our excellent Springfield-Mauser to a master gunmaker and have it made over into as fine a sporting rifle for American game as man could reasonably desire, the cost, all told, being in the neighborhood of forty or fifty dollars. They consider it rather absurd to put up with a fifteen or twenty dollar rifle to hunt moose or bear with, when they cheerfully pay fifty for a shotgun to hunt quail with. And certainly they get their money's worth.

Without finding fault with low-price rifles that "do the work" remarkably well, let us consider the points of a thoroughly well made rifle which can be turned out at a higher, but still reasonable, cost.

First, the barrel, which is by all odds, the most important part of the gun. In the day of black gunpowder our best rifle barrels were made from mild steel that was so soft it could fairly be cut

SPORTING FIREARMS

with a knife. Such metal was so easy to machine that good barrels could be turned out very rapidly and with little hand finishing; hence they were cheap, but shot as accurately as any. Smokeless powder required stronger material, and jacketed bullets required harder metal. This was supplied by the commercial nickle-steel of our day, harder to work than the soft steel it replaced, but still capable of being turned out in much the same way. Common nickle-steel will do for cartridges of the " medium game " class mentioned in a previous chapter; but when it is employed with ammunition of the " big game " or military class, there is trouble.

The trouble comes from erosion of the rifle bore. It has been assumed by riflemen generally that the erosion that cuts down the " accuracy life " of their barrels to a thousand rounds or so is caused by the excessive friction of jacketed bullets, unlubricated, driven at high speed through the rifle bore. If this were true, the wear would be fairly uniform throughout the bore, or might be greatest toward the muzzle, where the bullet gets its highest velocity. Such is not the case. Erosion always is greatest immediately in front of the neck of the chamber, where the bullet starts. Instead of being uniform, it begins with slight pits

MECHANISMS AND MATERIALS

which then are guttered out in irregular channels.

The gutters slowly deepen, and still more slowly creep forward up the bore. By the time they have advanced about two inches beyond the neck of the chamber they have deepened so much that a bullet leaving its cartridge shell has room to tilt before taking the rifling, and is deformed, perhaps has its jacket split, before entering the perfect part of the barrel. This damage is done by the gases of explosion of nitro powder, which are so hot that ordinary steel cannot stand the temperature. At first a little of this gas escapes around the bullet before it has gone far enough to seal the bore, and so the pits form. As the eroded portion extends, more gas escapes ahead, and more guttering results.

A barrel of ordinary nickle-steel will lose accuracy quite perceptibly after 1,000 rounds of the '03 U. S. ammunition (220-grain bullet), or even after 500 rounds, if the barrel happens to be a little above caliber. After, say, 3,000 rounds, it will shoot quite wild, notwithstanding that the forward nine-tenths of the bore may remain virtually intact. Such steel is strong enough to stand the breech pressure, and perhaps hard enough to resist bullet friction, but it will not stand the superheated gases of explosion.

SPORTING FIREARMS

The remedy, in so far as the gun is concerned, is two-fold. First a special compressed steel should be used, or a tungsten-steel, or other alloy that will resist the combined attack of friction and great heat. Second, the barrel should be throated so that the bullet fits as snugly as practicable at the start, and no other fit of bullet should be shot from that barrel. Both the superior steel and the extra work raise the price of the barrel, but the accuracy life of the rifle is greatly lengthened.

Many rifle barrels are soon ruined by excessive scrubbing with chemicals to remove metal fouling. By metal fouling is meant a deposit of hard metal from the bullet's jacket, which sticks with great tenacity, escapes observation for a time, but rapidly accumulates until the rifle shoots wild. Here, as with other diseases, prevention is better than cure. The gunmaker's part is extra care in finishing the interior of the bore, so that it shall be smoothly polished and true to gauge. It is not unlikely that a better material for the bullet jacket may be found than nickled steel, or cupro-nickle-steel—perhaps a bronze of high tensile strength that is a good anti-friction metal as well.

Ordinary lubricants will not work, because they are decomposed (disintegrated into their chemical

MECHANISMS AND MATERIALS

elements) by the great heat of explosion. Graphite alone will not stick to the bullet. Any inequality of action in a lubricant will make one bullet fly high and another low. Here is room for useful experiment. But in any case the barrel of a rifle that is to use the best modern ammunition should be of high quality and carefully gone over by an expert workman.

The bore of a rifle barrel should not have tight or loose places in it. Either it should be a true cylinder or, preferably, it should have a slight and even taper from breech to muzzle—say a quarter of a thousandth inch greater in front of chamber than at muzzle, in a .30 caliber. It can be tested by carefully pushing a well fitting lead bullet through the bore from breech to muzzle with a steel cleaning rod.

The muzzle is a rifle's most important part, and at the same time the one most exposed to injury by a chance blow or by unskilful use of the cleaning rod. Examine it with a lens. If lands and grooves are not perfectly cut to the very end, or if there be a burr of metal left at the mouth, or any sign of wear, reject the piece at once. Any imperfection here will allow gas to escape unevenly around the base of the emerging bullet and so tilt it at the critical moment of start.

SPORTING FIREARMS

A rifle barrel expands a good deal from the heat of firing, both around the bore and lengthwise. In order that this expansion should be even, the metal should be distributed symmetrically. There is no merit in an octagon or half-octagon barrel; rather the contrary. The best form is round and tapered toward the muzzle.

Every barrel flips or springs more or less at each discharge. So long as this flip is uniform, it may be allowed for in adjusting the sights; but grooves cut into the barrel for attaching sights, or other parts, affect the flip in a way that is detrimental to accuracy. There should be none. Some sporting rifles have a slot for forearm stuck almost directly under the rear sight slot. Such a barrel can be sprung with the two hands.

Some fine rifles have a matted rib extending along the top of the barrel to prevent the glare of sunlight from spoiling one's aim and to cut off the radiation of heat waves that arises from rapid firing. Such a rib, milled from the solid barrel, interferes with uniform expansion and contraction of the barrel, may even buckle it temporarily in continued firing, and the bore departs from a true circle. The difference probably will not be noticed in a sporting rifle, but no rib should be tolerated on an arm for match shoot-

MECHANISMS AND MATERIALS

ing. The matting is likely in time to aggravate the very trouble it was designed to cure, for when the bluing or browning wears off, as it will do much faster than from a smooth surface, the shooter's eyes will be annoyed by innumerable tiny facets of light.

All friction surfaces of a rifle's action should be polished to a mirror-like smoothness, so that there shall be no sticking, grating, or clattering in operating it. Bolts should be casehardened, small parts finished in a workmanlike manner, and bluing should be put on to stay. If economy must be practised, let it be in non-essentials, and not in the barrel that shoots or the mechanism that controls its shooting.

CHAPTER V.

RIFLE SIGHTS

HITHERTO we have been studying the rifle and its ammunition simply as engine and power, independent of the man behind the gun. Enter, now, the man, with his personal factor to be considered.

Cartridges, gun barrels, and breech mechanisms treat everybody alike. Not so the sights, trigger, and stock, which give one control over his weapon; these require adjusting to the individual, because men differ in eyesight, coördination, and build.

In very quick work, at close quarters, a rifle may be pointed like a shotgun, without seeing the sights at all. This kind of rifle shooting is so rare that we need give it scarcely a thought. The rifle, properly, is an arm of precision and must be handled as such, or we will miss. To hit a small object at short range, or a large one at long range, it is essential that the sights be exactly aligned and that the tip of the front sight barely touches,

RIFLE SIGHTS

or does not quite touch, the lower edge of the precise spot that one wants to hit.

A fine fore sight, covered by a hood, such as is made for target shooting, is not fit for hunting. It cannot be seen distinctly in varying light, nor in the shade of forests. A hunter's front sight must be open, strong, and firm, and its tip should be of some white or colored material that will show up plainly against a neutral or murky background.

The plain german-silver front sight generally sent out with a cheap rifle does not suit anybody's eyes. It is sure to glitter in sunlight. Take a rifle so fitted, stand out in the open, swing the gun to all points of the compass, and aim at various objects as you go. Besides the annoying glimmer, the appearance of the sight will vary according to the direction or angle at which light impinges on it. One side will show up clearer than the other, and you cannot well help aiming off to the clear side. The eye strain, too, will be excessive.

A black front sight is better, in good light, but it cannot be made out distinctly when the light is poor. A tip faced with platinum shows up fairly well, and it will not glitter like german silver. An ivory bead can be seen still more clearly, so long

SPORTING FIREARMS

as it is new and white, but it will turn yellow from the inevitable oiling, and then must be pared. One or two parings, and it is done for. Moreover, an ivory bead is brittle and easily damaged. The best all-round fore sight is a " gold " (alloy) bead. This shows up well, over snow as well as in dim places, yet does not glitter in the sun.

Fore sights with changeable beads are generally too frail and disconcerting for wilderness work. An exception may be noted in favor of what may be called a day-and-night sight. This consists of an ordinary " gold " bead sight to the base of which is hinged a steel standard bearing a large bead, or rather a small disk, faced with white enamel, which may be thrown up so that the white disk covers the ordinary bead. Such sights are made in Europe and should be copied or improved here, for there often come times in a hunter's experience when a sight that can be seen in the dusk would be appreciated. Imagine yourself with a bear or cougar treed at nightfall. If a luminous chemical can be found that will stand the weather, it might be better still for a facing.

In any case, a bead is preferable to a barleycorn, or knife-edge, or plain vertical bar, because, when aiming over an open rear sight, a round bead shows more clearly just how much front sight

RIFLE SIGHTS

is taken. Size of bead will be governed somewhat by length of rifle barrel and by local conditions. For general hunting, it is best to use the smallest bead that can be seen distinctly.

The rear sight usually attached to an American rifle of over .22 caliber, unless otherwise ordered, has two radical faults: first, its high wings cut off the view, not only below the thing aimed at, but on both sides. This is never desirable, and always is a nuisance when shooting at moving game. Second, the buckhorn is attached to a long, flat spring that runs back from the sight slot. This spring, in connection with steps (that never are adjusted for any range in particular), serves clumsily to elevate the rear sight—it takes two hands to operate the thing. Thereby the sight is brought too close to the eye for clear definition.

Any open rear sight will blur, more or less, because no eye can focus simultaneously on rear sight, fore sight, and mark aimed at. The closer it is to the eye, the more it will blur. Take the buckhorn out, tie it on the barrel three or four inches forward, and note the improvement. It is true that this shortens the sighting radius, but, of the two evils, blurred vision is much the worse.

A plain folding leaf sight, set directly in the

SPORTING FIREARMS

rear sight slot, is in better position, and is quicker to reset, than a buckhorn. The slot should be at least eleven inches ahead of the trigger, and preferably twelve. The reason that a military rear sight is only seven inches ahead of trigger is that it is generally used with the peep instead of the bar; in fact, I do not know any expert military shot who ever uses the bar, unless it be for quick firing.

The best of open rear sights is a plain, flat bar, with perhaps a small notch marking the center, and with one or two folding leaves for longer ranges than " point-blank." The bar should slant backward and have its top edge beveled, so as to offer a clear, clean outline in all lights. Its corners should be rounded, to prevent catching in gun case or other obstacles. The leaves should be held stiffly upright by springs, when in use; otherwise they will soon wear loose and can easily be jarred forward.

Whether the top of a bar sight should be plain or notched, with or without vertical line, and whether a notch should be wide or narrow, square, semi-circular, V-shaped, or U-shaped, are matters of personal choice. I can only state my own preference and the reasons for it.

To my eyes, a vertical line to mark the center

RIFLE SIGHTS

is unnecessary. If I pay any attention to it at all, I must change eye focus to do so, and this distracts me from my proper business of watching the mark. A triangle of ivory or platinum is worse, because it blurs with the bead of the fore sight. A deep notch is objectionable for hunting, because if I draw down into it (military "half sight") a great deal of the light is cut off. In the forest we need all the light we can get. Drawing half sight has this serious defect, for a hunter, that it is hard to do in quick aiming and may be impossible in dim light. Hence, if the rifle is adjusted for half sight, one is prone to overshoot.

I consider it bad practice to draw fine, medium, or coarse bead, according to distance. There is too much guesswork about it. With a high power rifle, you are almost sure to overdo the matter. So, on all accounts, I prefer a plain, level bar, with small nick to mark the center, and I always aim with full bead showing just its plain circle above the bar. When firing beyond the range for which bar or leaf is adjusted, I strive to aim as many inches higher as the drop of bullet requires. For instance, with a rifle using our military cartridge and bar permanently set for a "point-blank" of one hundred and fifty yards, I carry this simple rule in my head:

SPORTING FIREARMS

200 yards = 3 inches drop
225 yards = 5 inches drop
250 yards = 8 inches drop

Up to one hundred and seventy-five yards I make no allowance at all, as the variation does not exceed a couple of inches anywhere. It is easier to remember "three, five, eight," and aim accordingly, than to cut off precisely an infinitesimal fraction of an inch at the muzzle while looking keenly at the distant mark.

The method of attaching open sights to a rifle barrel is not of much moment with low power arms. With weapons using heavy charges that quickly heat the barrel to a sizzling temperature, it is quite another matter. The cheapest way to mount sights is in tapered slots dovetailed in the barrel. It is easy, then, to align the sights by tapping them over to right or left until a proper group is made. A slot weakens the barrel, and impairs its accuracy, if the barrel be thin and the charge heavy.

Sight blocks soldered or brazed to the barrel are liable to be knocked off when the weapon is hot from rapid firing. Smokeless powder makes the barrel expand quickly, while the block remains cool, and this strains the solder, or even tears it apart.

RIFLE SIGHTS

In rifles that have a rib on top of the barrel, milled from the solid metal, it is customary to dovetail the front sight slot lengthwise into muzzle end of rib. This prevents the sight from being knocked out of alignment. The objection is that individual rifles vary so that no standard position for the slot will suit them all, and no provision is made for adjustment sidewise.

The proper way to attach either a front or a rear open sight to a high power rifle is by a permanent band around the barrel, with movable sight base attached. We have a good example in the service arm of our army and navy, the Springfield-Mauser, commonly called "New Springfield." The front sight of this arm is pinned to a movable stud (*D, fig. 17*) which fits in a band (*A*) firmly attached to the barrel. Since

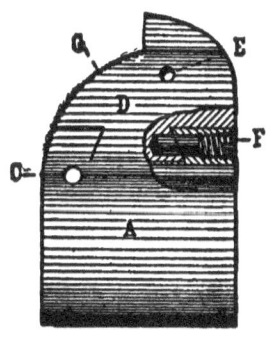 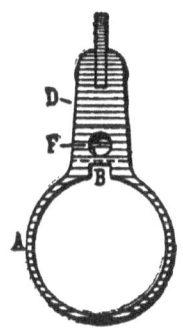

FIGURE 17.

SPORTING FIREARMS

no two rifles are exactly alike, each weapon is targeted by an expert, at the armory, until the correct position of its own front sight is determined. A hole is then drilled through base of movable stud into standing part of sight band, and a screw (F) is inserted, thus securing the front sight immovably in its place. The rear sight is attached by a similar band.

A peep sight on tang, frame, or cocking piece gives a longer sighting radius than an open sight on the barrel, with proportionally truer aim. The aperture of a peep sight for hunting should be considerably larger than that for target shooting. One's eye will center such a peep-hole instinctively, because the center of the hole gets more light than its edge. He will scarcely be conscious of using a rear sight at all.

In good light he can catch true aim quicker with such a peep than with any pattern of open sight, because there is no blur and because he need waste no time in cutting off the right amount of bead. He can see the whole object aimed at and a considerable space all around it. A distinct advantage of the peep over a plain open sight is that elevation can be adjusted to any range, and for any cartridge, with exactitude. One can set his " point-blank " to suit himself; he can use various

RIFLE SIGHTS

charges in the same gun without guesswork as to elevations.

An aperture of any kind is bothersome in the gray of dawn or twilight and in the murk of tall forests when the sky is overcast. To provide for shooting on such occasions (often one's best chance) there should be an auxiliary leaf sight on the barrel. Both it and the aperture must turn down out of the way of the other, for the two cannot be used together without blurring everything.

For target shooting and for hunting small game, the best position for a peep sight is on the tang. On a rifle of more power, a tang sight is not suitable, unless the arm is hammerless and its bolt retreats into the receiver, in which case a short tang sight can be mounted well forward, where it is not in the way of eye or hand. A peep is at its best when not more than two inches from the eye.

A bolt action rifle may have a peep sight attached to the receiver. This position is objectionable because it puts the aperture so far away that it is hard to center in dim light. To provide for this, there should also be a turn-down leaf on the barrel, as previously described. Unfortunately, nearly all patterns of receiver sights are made with the peep permanently erect. This should be remedied.

SPORTING FIREARMS

Receiver sights, as a rule are slow and awkward to reset at different elevations and the divisions are too coarse. A receiver sight that clamps in position merely by a lever is not sure to "stay put." By far the best sight of this class is the new Lyman for the Springfield-Mauser, operating by a milled-head screw.

A peep sight attached to the cocking piece has this advantage, that it draws back close to the eye, where it should be, in aiming, yet flies forward out of the way before the gun can recoil. I have used such a sight on a bolt action rifle with complete satisfaction. The anticipated variation from wobbling of cocking piece did not occur.

If one can afford it, the best possible combination of sights for open country is a "gold" bead front, permanent open rear with one leaf, and a telescope sight of the best modern pattern, the latter detachable in a moment, and ordinarily carried like a spyglass in leather scabbard slung from the shoulder. The open sights would be used for big game near by; the telescope for small game and for all long shots, running or standing.

Beware, however, of the old-fashioned telescope sight with long tube and delicate mountings, permanently attached to the barrel. It is not a practical instrument—not even for target shooting.

RIFLE SIGHTS

Its field (area visible through 'scope) is so small that one must grope and bob around to find his mark, and then can see but a short distance around it. If the object moves, he loses it.

The relief (distance from eye to eyepiece) is generally so short on such telescopes that the tube projects backward from the breech, forming a hook to catch in all manner of obstacles and quite unsafe to use on a rifle of much recoil. The lenses are easily jarred loose. The crosshairs are prone to break, or to separate in filaments when the weather changes. The adjusting screws stick out like sore thumbs, ever in the way of twigs and trouble. Such a 'scope is a delicate thing to carry, even to a rifle range, and is quite unserviceable in the field.

A modern telescope sight of good make is a short instrument (not over ten inches long, and some of them only six inches) that can be snapped on the rifle in a few seconds and detached as readily. It is sure to return to the same adjustment every time. Its construction throughout is strong enough for rifles of the highest power and for any kind of service—forest hunting, saddle work, or mountaineering—in short, it will stand what a spyglass will stand, and is as easily carried. Changes of elevation are made by a milled head operating the crosshairs, while the tube remains rigid. The mount is hollow, so that the open sights can be used, with telescope in position and without mounting the 'scope awkwardly on the side. The tube itself does not project back of the rifle's breech, but has a soft rubber eye-cup to cut off side light. It has a wide field and brilliant illumination, is adjustable to any eyesight, and corrects defects of vision.

It is a grave mistake to employ a high power in a rifle telescope. Five diameters should be the limit, for hunting, and three is more satisfactory all-round. The lower the power, the wider will be the field of vision, the brighter the illumination, and the less one's own tremor will be magnified, with consequent swaying of the image. A three-power 'scope makes an object three hundred yards distant appear only one hundred yards away, and that is good enough. The field of a good prism telescope of three-power is seventeen yards at one hundred yards, and is proportional at other distances. This means that, in aiming, the object is magnified to three times its apparent height to the naked eye, and that the shooter can see everything within seventeen feet of it at one hundred feet, or seventeen yards at one hundred yards.

An open sight cuts off the lower half of

RIFLE SIGHTS

field entirely; the telescope shows everything below, as well as above, and one can shift elevation at will, in the twinkling of an eye, by merely aiming high or low. It is an advantage to have stadia marks in the scope for this purpose. I once had a fifteen-inch .22 rifle, with telescope attached, that had dots on the vertical crosshair. Using long-rifle cartridges, it was easy to do very fine shooting at surprising distances. Notwithstanding the excessively high trajectory, one could catch any elevation he wanted. With this tiny gun, a ten-year-old boy made bull'seye after bull'seye at two hundred yards the first time he tried it, firing from muzzle-and-elbow rest, on a still day.

The extremely compact telescope sight now issued to expert riflemen in our army and national guard serves as a rough but practical rangefinder. When it was first brought out, a rifle equipped with it was tested by Captain Casey of the American team. A regular one thousand-yard target, with thirty-six inch bull'seye, had been placed so far away that the bull was a mere speck to the naked eye. Casey did not know the distance and set in to get the range for himself, by firing from the prone position. His first shot ricochetted into the target, scoring 3, the second was a 4, and the next eighteen bullets struck the

SPORTING FIREARMS

bull'seye, the wildest of them being no more than eighteen inches from dead center. The distance was then found to be *one mile*. The more one knows of rifle shooting, the better he can appreciate such a triumph for ammunition, gun, sight, and man.

CHAPTER VI

TRIGGERS AND STOCKS—CARE OF RIFLE

COMMAND of the trigger is the hardest and the most essential part of marksmanship. Few human operations require one's nerves to be so finely strung and his muscles so instantly responsive, in the face of immediate concussion and recoil. And the slightest blink or balk, quiver or flinch, when drawing trigger, will cause a miss.

The worst fault of cheap rifles is their rough and exasperating locks. Every man who is ambitious to excell with the rifle would gladly pay extra for a superior lock, if he could get it. Rifle makers offer many outside "extras" in the way of plating, engraving, and other non-essentials, up to hundreds of dollars, but the product of skillful handwork that buyers would most appreciate is a first-class trigger mechanism.

A lock made of inferior steel will soon wear out of adjustment. Then the trigger will creep, i. e., will start, stick, require two distinct pressures,

SPORTING FIREARMS

and go off unexpectedly at last. The language of anathema, even as perfected by Sterne in his *Tristram Shandy*, does not suffice to do such a mechanism justice. No man lives who can shoot decently with a creeping trigger.

In a rough lock, the notch into which the sear engages must be deep, lest the metal wear off or snap off. This notch is toothed upward at an angle, so that the sear cannot merely slide out but must lift against direct pressure of the mainspring. If the notch is deep, the trigger cannot let off quick and sharp.

When shooting offhand, it is impossible for anyone to hold without tremor. The best a man can do is to touch off just as his front sight swings to the right spot. This takes the utmost nicety of judgment and instantaneous execution of it. An error of a fiftieth of a second, in firing, is likely to throw the shot wild. In this infinitesimal interval, the eye, and brain, and finger, and trigger, all must work together.

No firing mechanism can be operated, from start to finish, in a fiftieth of a second, except a finely adjusted set trigger. A plain trigger requires that preliminary pressure be applied, to take up all but the last few ounces of strain and that it be steadily held there until the critical instant;

TRIGGERS AND STOCKS

then the final release is let off in a flash. Whether the pull be light or heavy, it positively should be smooth in take-up and instantly responsive to the final let-off.

Set triggers are of three types; single, split, and double. The single set is put in action by pressing it forward with the thumb. It is not likely to wear well. The split trigger (called by the maker "double set") likewise has its rear half pushed forward to set. It lasts better, but has a rather annoying backlash. Both of these patterns are slow to operate. Much better than either is the old reliable double set of our earliest frontier days (now trade-listed as "schuetzen double set," because re-introduced by German-American target shooters). This consists of two triggers spaced well apart, as in a double gun. The forward trigger is set by drawing the rear one back to a click; hence the arm can be set and fired very quickly, with gun to shoulder. A *well made* double trigger can be regulated to a hair, will always stay so, and will not jar off. In the hands of a cool man who is used to it, this is by far the best mechanism for deliberate offhand shooting, both at targets and at game in the open. As a nail-driver with the first shot, it has no equal.

A set trigger is unfit for quick repeating. Of

SPORTING FIREARMS

course, the front trigger can be used without setting, but the difference between the one-ounce set pull that one has grown accustomed to and the seven-pound unset pull that he may want to use in an emergency will balk anybody. I have been used to the set trigger for twenty years and to plain triggers for twice that span, yet I cannot change from one to the other without a little practice, nor do I know anybody else who can.

In fine, a set trigger is admirable for hunting small game, and for stalking on the plains or amid thinly forested mountains. It is an advantage when one uses a telescope sight. Yet for average hunting in forest and thicket and for all quick firing, it is out of place. One must choose according to the work he is to do.

At the other extreme is the old-fashioned military pull of from eight to twelve pounds. Very few men can ever be trained to do good offhand work with such a pull; nor does the accomplishment, when acquired, stand for anything meritorious—it is against nature. The modern military pull is better. It has, first, a dragging take-up of enough finger-power to make it safe among massed troops, then a comparatively light let-off. It will balk a recruit, in quick firing, until he gets used to it.

TRIGGERS AND STOCKS

The best all-round trigger for a sporting rifle is a plain one of from two to three pounds. If the lock is well made, there is no valid objection to a two-pound pull, and most men will do better shooting with it than with a heavier one. The lock parts should be of hard but tough steel, ground and polished smooth, and then adjusted by someone who is more of a watchmaker than a blacksmith.

A rifle should balance about four inches in front of the trigger guard. Good balance makes a gun buoyant and quick to swing into position, whereas an ill-balanced arm causes one to boggle and hunt for his sights. A well proportioned gun is less burdensome to carry than a clumsy one that may be a pound or two lighter.

No rifle using modern ammunition need have a barrel more than twenty-four inches long. Exhaustive tests by our ordnance department have proven that the muzzle velocity of a .30 Springfield-Mauser with a twenty-four inch barrel is but eighty-seven feet a second less than that of a thirty-inch barrel, while the accuracy of the short barrel is equal to that of the long one, its weight three-fourths pound less, the balance better, the arm more easily manipulated, and its total length suitable for cavalry as well as infantry. A differ-

SPORTING FIREARMS

ence of eighty-seven feet in muzzle velocity does not seriously affect the weapon's trajectory within sporting ranges. It is more than compensated by the merits gained. On the other hand, twenty-four inches is as short as a sporting barrel should be, unless for special service, because a shorter barrel is hard to aim truly without a telescope.

The weight of a high power rifle should be governed chiefly by the amount of free recoil set up by its cartridge. From seven and one-half to eight pounds is enough rifle weight for such a cartridge as the .30 U. S. A., '06, which gives a free recoil of fifteen foot-pounds, and six pounds is plenty for a .30-30 of seven pound recoil. However, it is here assumed that the weight is where it belongs—chiefly in action and breech end of barrel. A well made rifle has no superfluous wood or metal anywhere. A cheap one has a great deal of useless steel in the frame and elsewhere, that could be milled out to the betterment of the piece. I also assume that the best barrel steel is used, with no slots to weaken it, and that the piece has a shotgun butt to distribute recoil.

The fit of a rifle stock is not of so much consequence in firing deliberately with light charges, but a rifle that must be swung smartly into position for a shot on the jump should " come up "

TRIGGERS AND STOCKS

like a well proportioned shotgun. The stock of a sporting rifle, though, should be a little shorter than that of a shotgun, because the arm is sometimes used in prone position. Moreover, a rifleman's proper poise, when shooting offhand, is more erect and straight-necked than that of a gunner; hence the rifle stock needs more crook than a shotgun's. (Compare figures in Chapter IX.)

The following dimensions for rifle stocks are copied, in the main, from the writings of Mr. E. C. Crossman, an expert whose judgment in everything pertaining to rifled firearms deserves close attention.—

A rifle stock for a man of average build should measure about thirteen and three-fourths inches from trigger to hollow of butt; drop from line of sight to comb, one and seven-eighths inches; drop to heel, three inches. A short man, or one with short arm-reach, needs a shorter stock, say thirteen and one-half inches; a tall or long armed man, a longer one, fourteen or fourteen and one-fourth inches. A short neck requires a drop of one and three-fourths inches at comb and two and three-fourths inches at heel; long neck, two, and three and one-fourth inches, respectively.

If the stock is made to order, a cast-off (stock

SPORTING FIREARMS

bent away from face) of one-fourth inch at heel will help to bring the eye straight in line with the sights, without effort. A broad chested, full-faced man needs more. A well-shaped cheek piece also helps one to align quickly and naturally along the axis of the barrel, but adds weight to the gun.

A full pistol grip aids holding, provided it be close to the trigger and well curved (for an average hand, four inches from trigger to front of grip cap). A grip so shaped lessens the strain on the three grasping fingers and thereby leaves the trigger finger mobile for its proper work. A grip of four and three-fourths inches circumference fits a medium hand.

The conventional American rifle butt, slender, thin, and crescent shaped where it fits the arm, is a relic of the eighteenth century. It was properly designed for the rifles of that day, which had excessively long barrels and practically no recoil; hence were shot from the arm instead of from the shoulder. It is quite unsuitable for present-day weapons that use heavy charges and must often be handled quickly. A shotgun butt, slightly hollowed between heel and toe, comes promptly to the aim, does not catch in clothing, and its broad plate distributes recoil over a con-

TRIGGERS AND STOCKS

siderable area of the shoulder. A butt plate of hard rubber is too brittle; it is better of steel, checkered to prevent slipping when the shirt or coat is wet.

I like a trap in the plate, opening into a chamber within the butt where a jointed cleaning rod is kept, together with a spare striker or firing pin, spare springs (if flat), a folding screwdriver like that of our army, and a bullet jacket extractor. I much prefer a cleaning rod, even if many-jointed, to a pull-through thong. The latter is a poor excuse for cleaning and is liable to break, in which case it is a desperately hard thing to get rid of. Again, if a shell neck or a bullet jacket lodges in the barrel, the rifle is put out of action until a rod can be found.

Straight-grained walnut is stronger than figured wood. See that the grain runs lengthwise of the grip. Italian walnut is hardest and handsomest, but heavy. English walnut is next choice. A varnished stock is garish when new and shows every scratch and bruise thereafter, The most tasteful and durable finish is produced by several coats of linseed oil, each thoroughly rubbed in by hand.

The stock of a good rifle is improved by neat and sharp checkering on grip and forearm, to

SPORTING FIREARMS

keep the hands from slipping. It is well, also, to checker the trigger, safety catch, under side of bolt head, and butt plate. All other metal parts should be left severely plain, the blueing being of a dull finish. Anything that glitters on a rifle disturbs aim and alarms game by flashing like a heliograph. Many a time, the first notice I have had that another hunter was in the field came from the glitter of his rifle barrel.

Plating and engraving are out of place on a weapon that is not meant for ballrooms or dress parade. They cheapen and vulgarize it, as diamonds do a street costume. The beauty of a rifle is in its symmetry, its graceful contours, its easy poise in the owner's hands, its evident fitness for stern and manlike work. Let it show in every line and on every surface that it is no plaything, but a weapon of precision.

When one gets a good rifle, by all means let him take thoughtful care of it. This means work at times when one is least inclined for it; but *do* it. Never leave a rifle fouled from the day's shooting. A few nights' neglect, or even one, can ruin the best gun a man ever put to his shoulder.

The corrosive residue of smokeless powder cannot be removed with a wet rag, like that of black

TRIGGERS AND STOCKS

powder. The black carbon fouling that you see when looking through the barrel may be swabbed out with a dry wiper, but that is not what does the mischief. There is left a sticky residue that you cannot see, but that you can feel adhering to the wiper as you run a rod through. This has an acid reaction and attacks steel virulently. Water will not dissolve it. You must use either a nitro-solvent oil or an alkali, preferably the former.

Get a yard or two of firm cotton flannel, thick enough so that the tip of the rod will not push through it (a stuck rod is hard to remove). From this cloth cut square wipers of such size that they will just fit snugly but can be pushed through without strain. If your rifle is of such model that it can be cleaned from the breech (every rifle should be) open the breech, remove bolt, if there is one, put a newspaper on the floor, stand the rifle on it with muzzle down, and keep it so. Shove a dry wiper through, as far as it will go, and withdraw it. This brings out the carbon fouling.

Then saturate a wiper with nitro-solvent oil and swab the bore with it four or five times. Repeat with a fresh rag wet with the solution. Finally, turn the rifle up and clean out the muzzle

SPORTING FIREARMS

with a similarly oiled rag on the end of a sharpened pine stick, and the chamber with the same. In this way there is no chance of injuring the muzzle, which is the most delicate part of a gun.

It is not necessary to scrub hard, because your object is not to remove the sticky fouling by friction (it can't be done, not even with a wire brush), but to " dope " the barrel thoroughly with the solvent, and then give the latter time to get in its work.

Set the gun away for twenty-four hours. Then look through it. You may be surprised to see the bore evenly coated with a reddish deposit that looks like rust. It is not rust, but is something that soon will cause rust if you don't remove it. This deposit will appear, no matter how much elbow-grease you may have used on the barrel in the first place. When a gun is fired with smokeless powder, the gases are driven into the very pores or texture of the steel, and some of their acid residue is lodged there. This substance will " sweat out " gradually.

Now go for it, with the nitro-solvent, just as you did before. And repeat this operation the third day, even the fourth, if you love your gun. When a dry rag will come out perfectly clean, you may be satisfied that the gun is " surgically

TRIGGERS AND STOCKS

clean"—the microbes of rust have been exterminated.

Then oil the bore with liquid vaseline (albolene, cosmoline oil). This is absolutely neutral, cannot gum or turn rancid, and is thick enough to stay where it is put. A thin oil is not the thing for a gun bore, because it will run down into the chamber and leave the upper bore unprotected. If the rifle is to be put away for a long time, or if you live at the seashore, use mercuric ointment instead of oil; it is the best of all rust preventers.

You can make a good nitro-solvent cheaper than you can buy it from a sporting goods dealer. This is Dr. W. G. Hudson's formula, and a good one:

> Kerosene oil free from acid.......2 fluid ounces
> Sperm oil........................1 fluid ounce
> Spirits of turpentine.............1 fluid ounce
> Acetone ....1 fluid ounce

Your druggist can test the kerosene for you, in a jiffy, with litmus paper. The above solvent is a good rust-preventive.

If nitro-solvent cannot be procured, dissolve washing soda (not baking soda) until the water will take up no more (i. e., a saturated solution). Use this just as you would the solvent, but when through, carefully remove all trace of it from

SPORTING FIREARMS

the bore with dry rags, or the soda itself will set up rust. Then oil.

A cleaning rod to be used in a high power rifle is best made of steel, because grit will stick to a wooden rod, or even a brass one, and act on the bore like a rat-tail file. Any rod, whether wood or metal, will injure the muzzle in a surprisingly short time, if the wiping is done from the muzzle and in an unskilful way. The proper shape for a rod head is shown in the accompanying cut, which I have borrowed from Lieutenant Whelen's *Hints to Military Riflemen.*

RIGHT SHAPE FOR CLEANING ROD.

While a rifle cannot be cleaned thoroughly with a pull-through or field wiper, still, such treatment is better far than neglect. A common cord or thong is likely to break, and then the shooter is "hung up" for sure. A superior field cleaner, home made, was recently described by Mr. R. A. Kane:

"Get about three feet of heavily braided brass picture hanger's wire, drop a little soft solder on each end to keep it from raveling, then with a pointed tool like a carpenter's awl, separate the strands squarely in the middle, an inch from one

TRIGGERS AND STOCKS

end, and again twice more at intervals, leaving an inch between the openings. Into these openings through the braided wire insert oblong strips of cotton flannel thick enough to fit the bore snugly.

"To wipe the barrel, thread the plain end of the wire through from the muzzle and, as it appears at the open breech, take a turn around the hand and draw through smartly with a single pull. This excellent pull-through wiper is not liable to break off in the barrel and, when coiled up, may be carried in one's vest pocket. The wiping rags should be passed through the braided wire at right angles to each other."

Always wipe out the oil from a rifle bore before firing, for it will make the bullet fly wild. For the same reason, never wet or oil a bullet.

The mechanism of a rifle, wherever metal parts rub together, should be kept lightly oiled with a good thin oil like "3-in-1." Too much oil only serves to catch dust and grit. For the outside of the gun, Lieutenant Whelen advises that a piece of buckskin be saturated with oil; "once thoroughly saturated, it will last a lifetime, and is a great saver of oil." Of course, the gun first must be wiped thoroughly dry. The stock needs attention, at intervals, lest moisture get into it and swell it. Apply a coat of raw linseed oil, nothing else, and polish by rubbing with the hand.

To remove metal fouling, dope the barrel for three or four minutes with a preparation sold for the purpose, or with strongest ammonia, cleaning thoroughly thereafter till all trace of the alkali has vanished, and being especially careful to get none of the liquid in the action, for it is sure to cause rust.

If a rifle barrel once becomes pitted from rust, throw it away and get another. To try to remove rust with flour of emery or pumice would ruin the barrel anyway. Never polish any part that is blued. Do not put your rifle away with a cork or oiled rag in the muzzle: instead of keeping moisture out of the barrel it will seal up the moisture of the air inside the tube, and rust will follow.

It sometimes happens that the neck of a shell is blown up into the barrel, or a bullet jacket may lodge there. To remove either, insert a bullet jacket extractor, such as is issued to troops in the company repair kit, and tap out with a cleaning rod; or, upset one end of a bit of copper rod to full caliber of bore, insert small end down, and tap out gently.

PART II
THE SHOTGUN

CHAPTER VII

SHOT PATTERNS AND PENETRATION

IN passing from rifles to shotguns, we encounter a quite different set of problems. Still, the two arms have this much in common, that all depends upon what we want to do with them. Some kinds of gunning require a wide spread of shot at close quarters; others, a compact swarm at a considerable distance, Some game can be killed with small shot; other game requires large pellets. The more pellets we use, the better chance of hitting, but the more lead thrown, the heavier our gun must be. Charge of powder and shot must be proportional to weight of gun, and weight governs dimensions.

Let us take up one point at a time, keep our minds on it for the time being, and not be overhasty about drawing conclusions. In the end, we shall find that desirable qualities conflict, more or less, and that compromises between them must be made, lest we pick out a freak gun that excells in some one merit at the expense of others.

SPORTING FIREARMS

The power of a shotgun is determined by its pattern and penetration. Pattern means two things.—

1. The percentage of shot pellets that the gun will place in a given area, at a given distance, the standard being a thirty-inch circle at forty yards;

2. The evenness with which the pellets are distributed over that area.

An ideal pattern would be one containing every pellet of the charge, all spaced equidistant from each other. But no gun ever shoots that way. Many pellets are battered out of shape by concussion, or by friction against the bore. Since these offer unequal surfaces to the air's resistance, they soon swerve like a flat stone. Others are jostled out of the way by their crowded neighbors.

The pattern that a charge of shot will make depends very much upon how the gun barrel is bored. When shot are fired from a true cylinder they soon scatter widely, so that only thirty per cent to thirty-five per cent of the pellets will strike inside a thirty-inch circle, at forty yards. This is too thin a pattern for any but the shortest ranges; consequently guns are not bored to a true cylinder for sporting purposes. What are called

PATTERNS AND PENETRATIONS

"plain cylinders" by the trade are really made with a slight taper toward the muzzle, which compresses the charge enough to pattern, on the average, about forty per cent. Try your 12-gauge "cylinder" and see if it is not about 13-gauge at the muzzle.

To produce still closer patterns, the gun bore must have a rather abrupt choke (constriction) near the muzzle, so as to jam the shot together at the instant of leaving the gun's mouth. The fuller the choke, the denser the pattern. A quarter choke (sometimes called "improved cylinder") averages about fifty per cent of the charge in a thirty-inch circle, at forty yards; a half or "modified" choke, about sixty per cent; a full choke, about seventy per cent; an extreme choke, from seventy-five to eighty per cent. These, at least, are the definitions that I shall follow. Gunmakers disagree a good deal among themselves in the meaning they give to such terms as cylinder, open bore, modified choke, full choke, etc. It would be better to discard such words altogether and describe the degree of constriction by the percentage of charge that the gun patterns at forty yards. A "full choked" gun is simply one that patterns about seventy per cent, regardless of its gauge and other dimensions. It may take a constriction of 0.04 inch to full choke a 10-gauge, and only 0.02 inch to full choke a 20-gauge, but both guns will throw the same percentage of their charges (say seventy per cent) into a thirty-inch circle at forty yards. Length of barrel has nothing to do with this.

Spread of charge depends largely upon choke. A full choke (seventy per cent) gun throws the effective part of its charge into a thirty-inch circle at forty yards; a half choke into a thirty-six inch circle; a quarter choke into a forty-two inch circle; a " cylinder " into a forty-eight inch circle. This is true of all gauges alike, notwithstanding what you may have been told to the contrary.

Different chokes are adapted to different purposes. It is with shotguns just as it is with rifles. No one gun can excell in all kinds of shooting. When one is hunting ruffed grouse in the woodlands, the game springs up from concealment with a *whir-r-r*, and it must be downed at once, or, in a second or so, it is gone. Such shooting demands a wide spread of shot at close quarters, both to increase the chance of hitting and to reduce the chance of mutilating. In trap shooting, on the other hand, and in wildfowling, it often is necessary to hit hard at a considerable distance,

PATTERNS AND PENETRATIONS

and this requires the close pattern given by a full choke.

The pattern tables commonly published in gun catalogues are not of much use in the field. They show nothing but estimated performances of various chokes, with all sizes of shot, at the one range of forty yards. Game is shot at all distances from fifteen to fifty yards, or upwards. One should know what his gun will do at all sporting ranges. So I think it worth while to print here the average patterns obtained by actual firing with some quarter choke, half choke, and full choke 12-gauge barrels, at five-yard intervals, from twenty-five to fifty yards, and with three different charges—standard duck, trap, and upland loads. The figures show the number of pellets within a thirty-inch circle at each range. At twenty yards, all of these chokes place the full charge inside a circle of that size.

12-GAUGE PATTERNS OF
DUCK LOAD,
3⅛ drams bulk smokeless, 1¼ oz. No. 6 chilled shot
(279 pellets).

Range in yards.	Quarter Choke nominal 50% at 40 yds.	Half Choke, nominal 60% at 40 yds.	Full Choke, nominal 70% at 40 yds.
25	234=84%	251=90%	265=95%
30	201=72%	229=82%	246=88%
35	173=62%	198=71%	223=80%
40	142=51%	170=61%	198=71%
45	106=38%	140=50%	167=60%
50	84=30%	106=38%	145=52%

SPORTING FIREARMS

12-GAUGE PATTERNS OF

TRAP LOAD,

3⅛ drams bulk smokeless, 1¼ oz. No. 7½ chilled shot (431 pellets).

Range.	Quarter Choke	Half Choke.	Full Choke.
25	362=84%	389=90%	410=95%
30	315=73%	358=83%	384=89%
35	267=62%	306=70%	345=80%
40	216=50%	263=61%	303=70%
45	155=36%	212=49%	246=57%
50	114=27%	151=35%	211=49%

12-GAUGE PATTERNS OF

UPLAND LOAD,

3 drams bulk smokeless, 1⅛ oz. No. 8 chilled shot (460 pellets).

Range.	Quarter Choke	Half Choke.	Full Choke.
25	386=84%	414=90%	437=95%
30	336=73%	382=83%	409=89%
35	281=61%	322=70%	363=80%
40	225=49%	271=60%	318=69%
45	161=35%	216=47%	258=56%
50	110=24%	147=32%	212=46%

Bear in mind that these figures are averages. Any gun will vary ten per cent between shots, and sometimes a good deal more, but the tables show what may fairly be expected in the long run. Other gauges, of same chokes, will make similar *percentages* at the various distances, with shot

PATTERNS AND PENETRATIONS

adapted to them. It will be observed that the smaller sizes of shot show a falling off, in pattern, at the longer ranges. This is because they lose momentum faster, and hence the pellets stagger and fly wild.

It is commonly agreed that on the average a bird must be hit by at least three shot, of suitable size, to ensure killing. We may say, then, that killing patterns for birds require not less than the following number of pellets within a thirty-inch circle, at maximum range:

```
Snipe, etc........................350 No. 9s or 8½s.
Quail ............................235 No. 8½s or 8s.
Large grouse, or small ducks........165 No. 7s or 6s.
Large ducks.......................120 No. 6s or 5s.
Geese or turkeys................... 60 No. 3s or larger.
```

Bearing these figures in mind and glancing back, now, at our tables, we can figure pretty closely the maximum effective ranges of various chokes, in 12-gauge guns, with upland loads and duck loads. Other gauges will be considered later.

Of course, killing pattern depends not only upon choke but upon gauge of gun, since the larger the gauge, the more pellets it will handle. But let us consider one point at a time, lest our minds wander and we confuse ourselves. Some guns make dense patterns and yet bunch the pel-

SPORTING FIREARMS

lets irregularly, leaving considerable spaces untouched. This fault may be due to excessive choke. At present there are few, if any, makers, who will guarantee even patterns of more than seventy per cent average. Any choke in excess of this is likely to make patchy patterns. Again, an extreme choke is prone to lead at the muzzle. As soon as lead begins to stick to the bore, the shot go to flying wilder and wilder. Hence the merit or demerit of a closely choked gun is not learned by firing a few shots at sheets of paper, but by testing it after a hundred rounds have been fired rapidly, as in trap shooting.

Gunmakers can easily bore barrels that will average seventy-five per cent for five test shots, yet it is only once in a blue moon that we find an arm that will keep this up in an all-day shoot, without frequent doctoring. Quite recently the eighty per cent gun has been announced. I feel like predicting that steady averages of over seventy per cent will not be attained by peculiar boring of the muzzle, but by improved ammunition and better chambering.

The shape of the cone, directly in front of the cartridge chamber, affects pattern, and so does the fit of shell. When the crimp is blown out of a paper shell, it must fit the cone smoothly

PATTERNS AND PENETRATIONS

and fill it, or there will be a jump and tilting of the wad. If the shell be too short for the chamber, or the cone too long, gas will escape ahead of the shot and will scatter the charge.

Cheap guns of full choke are likely to give patchy patterns, because they have not been retouched by the gun-maker after testing. If one must put up with a cheap gun, it is wise for him to select a half choke (I am speaking of 12-gauges), because what it lacks in closeness of pattern will be more than made up in evenness and uniformity of shooting.

A dirty, or leaded, or rusted bore is sure to sprinkle its charge; it may even ball some of the shot—weld them together into an irregular mass that will fly anywhere except where it is wanted. Balled shot account for many distressing accidents, where men have been injured at extraordinary distances, or when standing far out of the line of fire. They also explain how Epiphalet Snooks killed an eagle at one hundred and five measured yards, with number six shot, from grandad's muzzle-loader. He might have done the same thing with both eyes shut and while flinching out of his skin. And yet Epiphalet will brag about that gun to the end of his days and will have several fights for its dear sake.

SPORTING FIREARMS

Balling of shot may be caused by bad ammunition, or by a charge that does not fit the gun in hand. Too much powder, or wads that are not thick and springy enough have a like effect in a choke bore, whereas such a load would batter the shot and sprinkle it from a cylinder bore.

Some guns string out their shot in a thin procession, part of the pellets lagging as much as ten or fifteen feet in the rear. In such case the pattern might look all right on the target, but a fast flying bird could plunge through the charge and escape. Cylinder bores are prone to string their shot, or to make widely varying groups.

If the shot are too soft, or not spherical, or of mixed sizes, they will string and scatter badly, no matter what kind of gun they may be fired from.

It is more important that a gun should pepper the target evenly and that it should behave well all day, regardless of how hot and dry the air may be, than that it should make very close patterns when tested for a few rounds under favorable conditions.

Effective range depends not only upon how many shot hit the object, but also upon their penetration and the shock they impart. The killing power of a pellet of shot is much easier to deter-

PATTERNS AND PENETRATIONS

mine than that of a rifle bullet, since shot are spherical. If shot of all sizes are fired with *the same muzzle velocity*, then the bigger the shot the better it will maintain speed, the farther it will range, the harder it will hit, and the deeper it will penetrate. Size of gun bore has nothing to do with this. A 28-gauge will drive any size of shot (if it chambers properly) as hard as an 8-gauge, and no harder, provided the powder charges give both loads the same muzzle velocity. Penetration depends simply upon speed and weight and hardness of pellet. A 20-gauge may drive its shot a little faster than a 12-gauge because it uses relatively more powder; or because the 12-gauge may be squib-loaded and hence cannot burn its powder properly; but size of bore is not the determining factor. Both guns can be standardized to the same initial velocity—it is all a matter of loading.

With the favorite powder charges of to-day, regardless of gauge, the maximum killing ranges of various sizes of shot, on pigeons, are about as follows:

No. 6......55 yards.	No. 8½......40 yards.
No. 7......50 yards.	No. 9.......35 yards.
No. 8......45 yards.	No. 10......30 yards.

On small ducks, with standard duck charges,

SPORTING FIREARMS

number 6 shot have killing penetration up to fifty yards, and number 5 up to fifty-five yards, but five or ten yards less on large, full-plumaged ducks. In heavy guns using stiff charges, number 1 or B shot do steady execution on geese at fifty to sixty yards, and BB or BBB shot at sixty to seventy yards, while 4s or 3s will do the same on ducks.

Always use chilled shot. There are men who prefer soft ones because such pellets flatten more on game and make large wounds, when fired at short range. But soft shot lose much more in pattern and penetration than they gain in shocking power. They are easily deformed in the gun barrel, especially by choke bores—then they lag in the rear and fly wild. Moreover, they are more prone to ball and to lead a gun than hard shot.

The only objection to chilled shot is that they are somewhat lighter than soft lead pellets of the same size and hence lose a trifle in sustained velocity, range, and penetration. The fault could be overcome by hardening shot with mercury, instead of " chilling " it, but the difference in weight is rather trivial, anyway.

The sizes, weights, and names of shot, according to the " American standard," are shown below:

PATTERNS AND PENETRATIONS

SIZES OF SHOT.

Name.	Diameter.	No. to the oz. Chilled Shot.	No. to the oz. Drop Shot.
Dust.	.04 inch.	....	4565
No. 12.	.05 "	2385	2326
" 11.	.06 "	1380	1346
" 10½ Trap.	.065 "	1130	1056
" 10.	.07 "	868	848
" 9½ Trap.	.075 "	716	688
" 9.	.08 "	585	568
" 8½ Trap.	.085 "	495	472
" 8.	.09 "	409	399
" 7½ Trap.	.095 "	345	338
" 7.	.10 "	299	291
" 6.	.11 "	223	218
" 5.	.12 "	172	168
" 4.	.13 "	136	132
" 3.	.14 "	109	106
" 2.	.15 "	88	86
" 1.	.16 "	73	71
B.	.17 "	....	59
BB.	.18 "	....	50
BBB.	.19 "	....	42
T.	.20 "	....	36
TT.	.21 "	....	31
F.	.22 "	....	27
FF.	.23 "	....	24

COMPRESSED BUCKSHOT.

4 C	.24 inch	341 balls to lb.
3 C	.25 "	299 " " "
2 C	.27 "	238 " " "
1 C	.30 "	175 " " "
0	.32 "	144 " " "
00	.34 "	122 " " "
000	.36 "	103 " " "

It is unfortunate that some shot manufacturers use antiquated standards of size and nomenclature, which lead to confusion.

SPORTING FIREARMS

Buckshot cannot be recommended for any sport; they cripple more deer than they kill, except at very close quarters. They may be useful, however, for defensive purposes. For choke bores, they should be selected by chambering in the muzzle. Push a wad down into the closest part of the choke, and observe whether a layer of the shot will pass it without jamming.

If a shotgun is ever used on large game, it should be only with solid ball and at close quarters. The ball must fit properly in the narrowest (tightest) part of the gun bore. The actual calibers of true cylinders are as follows:

10-gauge, 0.775 inches.   16 gauge, 0.662 inches.
12-gauge, 0.729 inches.   20-gauge, 0.615 inches.

Proper sizes of round ball for cylinder bores, allowing for patch, are:

10-gauge, 0.760 inch, 630 grains.
12-gauge, 0.714 inch, 540 grains.
16-gauge, 0.647 inch, 390 grains.
20-gauge, 0.600 inch, 300 grains.

Chokes amount to from 0.01 to 0.04 inch, depending upon caliber and upon pattern desired. To allow for full chokes, our factories load ball cartridges with undersized bullets, the weights being as follows: one and one-eighth oz. ball for

PATTERNS AND PENETRATIONS

10-gauge; one oz. for 12-gauge; seven-eighths oz. for 16-gauge; five-eighths oz. for 20-gauge.

Such missiles have great smashing power, at short range, and will carry straight enough for deer shooting up to forty yards. At one hundred yards they will generally miss a stable door, and the stable itself at two hundred yards, unless E. Snooks is at the trigger.

CHAPTER VIII

GAUTHES AND WEIGHTS

THE killing pattern of a shotgun depends not only upon choke but upon gauge. For example, if we take a 12, a 16, a 20, and a 28-gauge, all of them full choked (seventy per cent), and load each with its standard charge of number 8 shot, they will pattern as follows:

12-gauge uses 1⅛ oz.=460 pellets, and patterns 70%=322.
16-gauge uses 1   oz.=409 pellets, and patterns 70%=286.
20-gauge uses ⅞ oz.=358 pellets, and patterns 70%=251.
28-gauge uses ¾ oz.=307 pellets, and patterns 70%=215.

Each gun throws seventy per cent of its charge into a thirty-inch circle, at forty yards, but the 12-gauge plants nine shot where the 16-gauge places eight, the 20-gauge seven, and the 28-gauge six. The bigger the bore, the more pellets it will handle, of a given size, and the denser will be its pattern, if chokes are the same.

On the other hand, if we load all four guns with the same number of pellets, but still give each gauge its standard weight of lead, then, the bigger the bore, the larger pellets it will handle, and the greater will be its effective range.

GAUGES AND WEIGHTS

We can simplify the discussion of gauges by means of a table that one's eye can take in at a glance. I give, below, average forty-yard patterns of guns of all gauges from eight to twenty-eight, and various chokes, with standard loads of all sizes of shot from BBs to 9s, omitting such figures as are of no practical use. Chilled shot are employed in all cases, except Bs and BBs. (For number of pellets to the ounce, see previous chapter.) The charges here tabulated are:

2 ounces. Heavy 8-gauge.
1½ ounces. Heavy 10-gauge.
1¼ ounces. Heavy 12-gauge.
1⅛ ounces. Medium 12-gauge. Heavy 16-gauge.
1 ounce. Light 12-gauge. Medium 16-gauge. Heavy 20-gauge.
⅞ ounce. Light 16-gauge. Medium 20-gauge.
¾ ounce. Light 20-gauge. Medium 28-gauge.

AVERAGE SHOT PATTERNS,
30-inch circle, 40 yards.
FULL CHOKE GUNS=70%.

Shot	2 oz.	1½ oz.	1¼ oz.	1⅛ oz.	1 oz.	⅞ oz.	¾ oz.
BB	70	50					
B	83	70	52				
No. 1	102	76	64	57			
2	123	92	77	69	62		
3	153	114	97	86	76	67	
4	190	143	119	107	95	83	71
5	241	181	151	135	120	106	90
6		234	195	176	156	137	117
7		314	262	235	209	183	158
7½			302	272	242	211	181
8			358	322	286	251	215
8½				390	347	303	260
9				461	410	358	307

SPORTING FIREARMS

HALF CHOKE=60%.

Shot. No.	1¼ oz.	1⅛ oz.	1 oz.	⅞ oz.	¾ oz.
5	129	116			
6	167	151	134	118	
7	224	202	179	157	135
7½	259	239	207	181	155
8	307	276	245	215	184
8½		334	297	260	223
9		395	351	307	263

QUARTER CHOKE=50%.

Shot. No.	1¼ oz.	1⅛ oz.	1 oz.	⅞ oz.	¾ oz.
6	140				
7	187	168			
7½	216	194	174		
8	256	230	205		
8½		279	248	217	
9		329	293	256	220

"CYLINDER"=40%.

Shot. No.	1¼ oz.	1⅛ oz.	1 oz.	⅞ oz.	¾ oz.
7	150	134			
7½	172	155	138		
8	204	184	164	143	
8½		223	198	173	
9		263	234	204	176

Referring back, now, to the preceding chapter, where killing patterns for various birds are tabulated, the reader can see for himself what gauges and chokes and sizes of shot are effective at forty yards, with customary charges as shown above. Good estimates of performances at other ranges, from twenty to fifty yards, may be made by comparing the work of 12-gauges (see Chapter VII), at forty yards, with those of other gauges shown

GAUGES AND WEIGHTS

here, and making proportional allowances, according to charge of shot.

We see at once that size of shot should be regulated to gauge of gun, as well as to size of game. With standard charges, neither a 20-gauge nor a 16-gauge will pattern close enough for ducks, (at forty yards) with any shot larger than number 6; whereas a 12-gauge (full choke, of course) will handle 5s effectively; a 10-gauge, 4s; an 8-gauge, 3s. Similarly, a 20-gauge will make a forty yard goose pattern with 3s; a 16-gauge with 2s; a 12-gauge with 1s; a 10-gauge with Bs; an 8-gauge with BBBs. Consequently, if other things are in normal proportion, the bigger the bore, the farther it will kill.

Of course, a small bore can be so built and so loaded as to handle a charge that is "standard" for a bigger gauge; but would we gain or lose by it?

The narrower the bore, the longer the column of shot will be, with a given charge. This means increased friction in the small bore, greater tamping of the powder and consequently quicker burning, greater breech pressure, and a more violent recoil. Moreover, small bores generally are loaded with finer shot than large bores, when used for the same purpose; and the finer the shot, the

SPORTING FIREARMS

harder the gun will kick. All experts, I believe, agree that small bores require more gun weight in proportion to shot weight than large bores do. For example, a 12-gauge using two and three-fourths drams of powder and an ounce of shot need not weigh over six and one-fourth pounds, but a 16-gauge charged with similar load should be half a pound heavier; and a 20-gauge, another half pound. Since the prime merit of a small bore is its lightness of gun and of ammunition, it must be apparent that overcharging such a weapon is poor policy.

Hitherto we have been speaking only of shot loads, irrespective of powder. Would anything be gained by using light loads of shot and heavy charges of powder?

We hear a good deal, nowadays, about small-bore "express" shotguns—a term borrowed from the riflemen's parlance of thirty years ago. Anyone can see that if the velocity of shot can be raised, say, two hundred feet a second, without spoiling the pattern, then their effective range will be greater, and a gunner need not allow so closely for "lead" of his bird, nor for drop of shot at long range.

Of course, it is easy to increase the velocity by using more powder, but the trouble is here, that

GAUGES AND WEIGHTS

with present systems of gun boring and present methods of cartridge making, any considerable increase above standard charge of powder is likely to batter the shot, lead the gun, and ruin the pattern. We cannot have successful high-velocity shotguns until makers of guns and of ammunition consent to spend a good deal of time and money on something new—and this, naturally, they are loath to do.

Tentative experiments have been made, with encouraging results. It is claimed that a seven and one-half pound 12-gauge has been built in England that brings down overhead ducks from an *altitude* of fifty to sixty yards. Quite recently, Mr. Charles Askins, the gun expert, has secured an American eight pound 16-gauge in which he uses three and one-fourth drams of Schultz and an ounce of shot, " probably the highest-velocity load ever regularly shot from an American shotgun." The astonishing thing about this gun and charge is that they make an even pattern of eighty per cent. It will be interesting to learn whether this sturdy weapon behaves well at the fiftieth or hundredth round.

The advantage of high initial velocity is greater with large shot than with small ones, because the latter are less able to *maintain* speed. Extra

SPORTING FIREARMS

powder charge, with fine shot, is wasted, just as an athlete's strength would be wasted in trying to throw grains of sand to a distance. Still, it seems feasible to give number 7 shot a somewhat higher remaining speed at duck ranges than 6s have with their present standard charges of powder, and number 9 shot a higher remaining speed at quail ranges than 8s now have. When this is accomplished, the six and three-fourths pound 20-gauge of the future will be as effective with seven-eighths ounce of shot as our seven and one-half pound 12-gauges of to-day are with one and one-eight ounce, as regards *both* spread and density of pattern. Of this, more anon.

We may now take up the four classes of shotguns, seriatim, namely: upland, wildfowling, trap, and all-round guns.

1. *Upland Guns.*—For hunting snipe, plover, woodcock, quail, and the larger grouse, we do not need very powerful arms, but light weight of gun and ammunition are essential. When a man has tramped the fields from morn till noon with a seven and one-half pound gun, he will be in ready mood to swap for something lighter. Five yards greater killing range does not compensate for stiff muscles and the lassitude that comes from overexertion. A tired man is too slow.

GAUGES AND WEIGHTS

There is an opposite extreme to be avoided: the feather-weight. A certain weight is required to steady one's swing. Men of average physique will make fewer misses, in an all-day hunt afield, with a gun weighing between six and seven pounds, than they will make with either a heavier or a lighter arm.

Now, what power is needed for upland shooting? and can we get it in such light guns? and what kind of gun will give us the most power with the least fatigue in handling it?

Nine-tenths of upland game is killed within thirty-five yards. Any gun that will make the minimum killing pattern at forty yards (say 235 number 8 shot within a thirty-inch circle) has ample power for the purpose. This is done by a quarter-choke with one and one-eighth ounce of shot, by a half-choke with one ounce, and by a full choke with seven-eighths ounce, regardless of gauge. So much for long range.

But we also must have, for upland work, an open pattern at short range. How short a range? Not fifteen yards, because, at that distance, a forty per cent cylinder bore will bunch its full charge within a ten or twelve inch circle, and blow a bird to pieces, or at least make it unfit for table. At twenty yards, then? Yes, at twenty

SPORTING FIREARMS

yards we want a pattern that will not mangle. This we can get with a cylinder bore using one and one-eighth ounce of shot, with a quarter-choke using one ounce, or with a half-choke using seven-eighths ounce.

Hence our conditions are met by a light 12-gauge with right barrel cylinder bored and left barrel quarter-choked; also by a 16-gauge of quarter and half-choke; also by a 20-gauge of half and full-choke.

We now are on the firing line of what has sarcastically been called "the battle of the bores." Let us compare the guns last named, testing them side by side, for spread and density of pattern, both at average (twenty-five yard) and extreme (forty yard) upland ranges. First with number 8 shot.—

PATTERNS WITH NUMBER 8 SHOT.

25 yards.

Gauge.	Charge of No. 8 shot	Killing Circle. Right.	Left.	Pattern. Right.	Left.
12	1⅛ oz.	30	26	368	386
16.	1 oz.	26	22	344	368
20.	⅞ oz.	22	18	322	340

40 yards.

Gauge.	Charge of No. 8 shot.	Killing Circle. Right.	Left.	Pattern. Right.	Left.
12.	1⅛ oz.	52	42	184	230
16.	1 oz.	42	36	205	245
20.	⅞ oz.	36	30	215	251

SPORTING FIREARMS

PATTERNS WITH NUMBER 8½ SHOT.

25 yards.

Gauge.	Charge of No.8½shot.	Killing Circle. Right.	Left.	Pattern. Right.	Left.
16.	1 oz.	30	26	396	416
20.	⅞ oz.	26	22	365	391

40 yards.

Gauge.	Charge of No.8½shot.	Killing Circle. Right.	Left.	Pattern. Right.	Left.
16.	1 oz.	52	42	198	248
20.	⅞ oz.	42	36	217	260

Comparing these figures with the preceding table, we find that, with suitable chokes, and normal loads, a 16-gauge using number eight and one-half shot excells a 12-gauge with number eight, up to forty yards; and that a 20-gauge gives a denser pattern, with killing circle only four inches less at twenty-five yards than the 12-gauge, under same conditions. If number nine shot were used, the guns might be bored more open, and still maintain killing patterns, but the effective range would be cut down to thirty-five yards.

For the larger grouse we must use larger shot and the patterns need be no denser than 165 at extreme range. Testing the small bores last mentioned (16-gauge cylinder and quarter-choke, 20-gauge quarter and half-choke) with number seven and one-half shot, we get the following averages, as compared with the 12-gauge.

GAUGES AND WEIGHTS

"Killing circle" refers to the area over which the shot spread uniformly, and "pattern" means the number of pellets within a 30-inch circle.

Anybody can see, from this, that at medium range the large bore has the advantage, if chokes are as here given; whereas at long range the smaller bores surpass it.

If we give the 16-gauge the same chokes as the 12, and give the 20-gauge a quarter choke right and half-choked left, then these small bores will do better at twenty-five yards, but will sprinkle too thin at forty yards—provided we stick to number 8 shot.

These are the reasons for conceding, as nearly everyone does, that small-bores are only for the expert who can center his bird time after time, and that they are poor weapons for ordinary marksmen, because their killing circles are too small.

Now comes up a point that seldom is considered. Up to forty yards, number eight and one-half shot have killing penetration for all upland game except large grouse. Suppose we try number eight and one-half in a 16-gauge with right-barrel a cylinder and left quarter-choke; also in a 20-gauge, right quarter-choke, left half-choke.—

GAUGES AND WEIGHTS

PATTERNS WITH NUMBER 7½ SHOT.

25 yards.

Gauge.	Charge of No.7½ shot.	Killing Circle.		Pattern.	
		Right.	Left.	Right.	Left.
12.	1⅛ oz.	30	26	310	326
16.	1 oz.	30	26	276	290
20	⅞ oz.	26	22	264	272

40 yards.

Gauge.	No.7½ shot.	Right.	Left.	Right.	Left.
12.	1⅛ oz.	52	42	155	194
16.	1 oz.	52	42	138	174
20.	⅞ oz.	42	36	151	181

If larger shot than number seven and one-half is used in the small bores, then our 16-gauge must be half-choked, and the 20-gauge full-choked, or the pattern will be too thin for any but short distances. Guns so choked are only for the expert marksman, and for open country at that. In ruffed grouse hunting, or brush work generally, they would be well-nigh useless.

I conclude, then, that for upland shooting a 16-gauge should be cylinder-bored (forty per cent) in the right barrel, quarter-choked (fifty per cent) in the left; a 20-gauge, quarter-choked in the right, half-choked (sixty per cent) in the left; and that both should be charged with number seven and one-half shot for ruffed grouse, or number eight and one-half for quail and the smaller birds. So built and so loaded, the small-bores

SPORTING FIREARMS

have all the spread and density and penetration that are needed for upland shooting. It follows that if they have, in addition, any peculiar merits which are lacking in the larger gauges, then these merits may well be determining factors in choice of weapon.

The advantages of light weight and handy grip they certainly do possess. Normal dimensions for upland guns of various gauges may be stated as follows.—

Gauge.	Weight.	Bbls.	Shell.	Powder.	Shot.
12.	7 lbs.	30 in.	2⅝ in.	3 dr.	1⅛ oz.
*16.	6¾ in.	30 in.	2 9-16 in.	2¾ dr.	1 oz.
16.	6½ lbs.	28 in.	2 9-16 in.	2½ dr.	1 oz.
*20.	6½ lbs.	28 in.	2⅞ in.	2½ dr	⅞ oz.
20.	6¼ lbs.	28 in.	2½ in.	2¼ dr.	⅞ oz.

(The guns starred (*) give a slightly higher velocity to the shot than standard.)

In comparing weights, we should consider ammunition as well as weapon. Twenty-gauge cartridges weigh three pounds less per hundred than those of 12-gauge.

I do not advise using shorter barrels than twenty-eight inch, in any gauge. A good length of sighting plane is essential for true alignment, and a certain length is needed for steady swing.

If a pump gun or self-loader is preferred, then, for the uplands, let it be a 12-gauge cylinder, or

GAUGES AND WEIGHTS

a 16-gauge quarter-choke, or a 20-gauge half-choke.

2. *Wildfowling Guns.*—Close patterns at long range are indispensable for ducks, geese, brant, and other waterfowl. Large shot must be used, and plenty of them. The powder charge should be as heavy as practicable, to drive the shot at good speed. The gun should be of large bore, full choke and heavy metal. It is true that small-bore guns of high velocity do good work on wildfowl under certain conditions, but only when handled by expert marksmen. Average duck hunters are badly handicapped by anything less than a heavy 12-gauge, say one of eight pounds, with thirty-two-inch barrels, using from three and one-half to three and three-fourths drams of powder, and one and one-fourth ounce of shot. Such a gun, charged with number 6 shot for inland ducks, or number 3s for geese, is a good killer up to fifty yards.

If greater range is desired, then choose a 10-gauge of nearly or quite ten pounds, thirty-two inch barrels, and taking shells long enough for five drams of powder, well wadded, and one and one-half ounce of 4s or 5s for ducks, 1s or 2s for geese. Properly held, it will account for nearly everything within sixty yards.

SPORTING FIREARMS

On the coast, where long shots may be the rule, an 8-gauge of thirteen pounds, thirty-four inch barrels, chambered for seven drams of powder and two ounces of 3s or 4s for ducks, 1s or BBs for geese, is eminently a proper arm for men who can wield it promptly. Its effective range is about seventy yards. A glance at the first table in this chapter will show the superiority of large charges and big shot, beyond peradventure. Still, it is likely that nearly all inland duck hunters will find a specially designed 12-gauge their most satisfactory arm, in the long run.

3. *Trap Guns.*—The standard trap gun of to-day, the world over, is a full-choked 12-gauge. Usually it is of seven and three-fourths to eight pounds weight, with thirty-two inch barrels, using three and one-fourth drams of powder, and one and one-fourth ounce of number seven and one-half shot. Both closeness and uniformity of pattern are indispensable.

4. *All-round Guns.*—The man who can own but one gun for all purposes, and whose shooting includes both upland game and waterfowl, should certainly buy a double-barrel for the sake of having two chokes, for short and long range respectively or else have two barrels for his auto. Since his weapon must be a compromise, he cannot lean

GAUGES AND WEIGHTS

toward any extreme, nor can he fairly expect to be a top-notcher in either form of sport. It is essential that his gun should throw large and small shot equally well. On this account more, perhaps, than on any other, a 12-gauge is pre-eminently the arm for him. Let it be quarter-choked (fifty per cent) in the right barrel, and full-choked (seventy per cent) in the left, chambered for two and five-eighths inch shells, so that either three, or three and one-eighth, or even three and one-fourth drams of powder may be used with one and one-eighth ounce of shot. Such a gun should weigh about seven and one-half pounds, and should have thirty-inch barrels.

If, however, the gunner's requirements never call for larger shot than number six; then a seven pound 16-gauge might answer every purpose.

CHAPTER IX

MECHANISM AND BUILD OF SHOTGUNS

REPEATING shotguns are cheap, serviceable, deadly, and therefore popular, in spite of their inherent ugliness. They are less objectionable at the traps than anywhere else. In duck shooting over decoys, where powerful charges are not needed, the 12-gauge pump gun gives a good account of itself. The only 10-gauge repeater on our market scarcely deserves mention, as it is too light to handle any duck loads that are strong enough to bring out the superiority of a ten over smaller bores. In upland shooting, a repeater is clumsier to carry than a neat double-barrel of equal power and has the marked disadvantage of only one choke for all ranges.

Self-loading shotguns—generally called " automatics "—are still in the awkward period of development. This much can be said for them: that they are positive self-ejectors, with single trigger, at a moderate price. From a mechanical

MECHANISM AND BUILD

standpoint their chief defect is a lurking uncertainty of functioning. At the time of this writing, such arms are only made in 12-gauge, with forearm so excessively deep as to throw the handhold too low for good instinctive pointing. It would be better to cut down the gun to 16 or 20-gauge, with lines proportionally refined, and stock it so that both of the shooter's hands will come up naturally in line when he aims.

There are other reasons for restricting the self-loader to small and graceful proportions. Nobody of good taste can tolerate a gun that looks like a crooked club and handles like one. Moreover, there is an ethical objection to rapid-fire arms that would be silenced if smaller gauges of narrow killing pattern were adopted. It is claimed that they are unsportsmanlike: that they tempt one to ruthless and indiscriminate slaughter. Automatic shotguns are outlawed in Pennsylvania and throughout Canada, on the same principle that forbids the use of swivel guns on waterfowl and dynamite on fish.

We may note certain inconsistencies in such legislation. If the self-loader is an unsportsmanlike weapon, then so is the pump gun; for there is little, if any, difference in their destructiveness, when used by skilled and unscrupulous hands.

SPORTING FIREARMS

It is not the gun, but the gunner, who is to blame. Our passenger pigeons were not exterminated with breech-loaders, nor our buffalo with self-loading rifles. And, to-day, far more game is slaughtered, in season and out of season, with single-loading "nigger guns" than with all the automatics in America. It is stated that about 500,000 new shotguns are sold every year in the United States, of which not less than 350,000 sell for $5, or less. Who uses those cheap guns? As a rule, they are in the hands of pot-hunters who sneak about, at all times of the year, murdering every edible animal that they can find, on the ground or any way they can get them. This irresponsible class of men and boys are too shiftless to keep a complicated gun in working order, even if they could muster the price. The only measures that can be counted upon to protect the wild life of this country are uniform game laws, decently paid wardens, national breeding grounds, and prohibition of the sale or import of dead game.

Regarding small bore automatic shotguns, I agree heartily with the views expressed by Mr. Askins, in a recent magazine: "It is not to be doubted that many conscientious hunters are prevented from using a magazine shotgun by the feel-

MECHANISM AND BUILD

ing that it is an unsportsmanlike arm; that it gives the marksman an undue advantage, is unnecessarily deadly. Such men would take most kindly to a 20-gauge with its closer choke, narrowed killing circle, and lessened charge of shot. In the opinion of these marksmen the reduced chances of killing with a single load would be exactly balanced by the reserve of fire." I may add that, on the score of sportsmanship, there is the same refined pleasure in getting results with light guns that we feel in landing big fish with delicate tackle. But nobody wants a 20-gauge repeater unless it is built throughout on 20-gauge lines.

Up to the present time, everyone who insists upon graceful contours, " live " balance, due proportions of gun to charge, fine materials throughout, and skilful hand finish, has no choice but a double gun. In double-barrel shotguns we can get—what we cannot get in rifles—anything we want, turned out by either of half-a-dozen American factories.

The best barrels, irrespective of price, are those made of fluid-compressed steel, either Krupp or Whitworth. Next in quality come the various " nitro " steels of high grade, for which each gunmaker seems to have his own pet name. They are homogeneous metals, of high tensile strength, that are drilled from short rods, then rolled and drawn, while hot, to the required length and rough-bore. Barrels of this sort are not only stronger than Damascus: they are of closer texture, they take a finer polish, and hence do not pit or lead so easily with smokeless powder. Besides, they are easier to make, and therefore cheaper. In the old days, Damascus was preferred because it was a certain guarantee of quality, as compared with the inferior plain steel of the period. Damascus is made from alternate layers of iron and steel, twisted together into a spiral, heated and hammered flat, welded around a mandrel, forged into shape, bored to gauge, and then browned by a rusting process so as to bring out the figure or " curl " of the metals. Such a barrel is so tough that it would bulge, rather than burst; but it is soft enough to be dented easily, and its iron portion is eaten into by the acid gases of smokeless powder.

Aside from the quality of metal and wood, a well-made gun is distinguished from a cheap one chiefly by the following points.—

1. The frame is comparatively light. Gun frames are milled from the solid block. If this job is skimped, a lot of superfluous metal is left at the breech, making the gun needlessly heavy and ill-balanced.

2. The working parts are of tough and homo-

MECHANISM AND BUILD

geneous steel, hard enough to stand long wear. They are finished by master craftsmen and have an unmistakably thoroughbred look, if we may apply such a term to inanimate material. In a cheap gun we find such abomination as "malleable casting." It is soft or brittle stuff, and every part grates on its bearings. Inside of a gun beauty is proof of utility, every time.

3. All joints are perfect. In the finest specimens of guns the doll's-head and other joints fit with such exquisite nicety that the lines of junction cannot be seen with the naked eye. A human hair, or the thinnest tissue paper, would prevent the barrels from closing on the breech. Similarly the fitting of wood to metal is so close that no moisture can seep in between them.

4. The trigger-release is smooth, quick, and invariable. This is a matter of the utmost imporance, for marksmanship with any kind of firearm depends more upon absolute control of the trigger than upon anything else. I would put up with almost any other botch in a gun rather than tolerate a "mean" trigger. The various grades of meanness can only be detected by firing, or snapping, repeatedly from the shoulder.

In the matter of trigger-pull, one can only express his own preferences, for what suits one man may disconcert another. If, after firing several rounds, you find yourself thinking of the trigger at all, then that lock needs doctoring to fit your personal equation. A pull of not under three and one-half pounds for the rear trigger is necessary, in any case, to preclude jarring-off of the second barrel. The front trigger should actually pull lighter than the rear one, because it has not so good leverage. Then both triggers will seem to pull alike.

Choice of single or double-trigger mechanism depends a good deal upon one's shooting habits. "It is hard to teach an old dog new tricks;" and yet the new trick may be a good one. Men who are not set in their ways will find a first-class single trigger an advantage, because one pulls it always from the same point, at the same angle, with the same pressure, and without relaxing his grip. A single trigger has this further merit: that in shooting heavy loads continuously, as at the traps, one's finger is not bruised by a front trigger recoiling against it, or by the guard. Everybody who has suffered in this way knows that it causes flinching. The difference in speed of fire, between single and double triggers, amounts to nothing, when stiff charges are used; for the kick-up and return of muzzle must be waited for, in any case. A left-

MECHANISM AND BUILD

handed shooter will find the single trigger easier to manipulate than double ones.

Hammerless guns are the safest, for the obvious reason that they cannot be discharged by catching in brush, clothing, fence wires, etc.; also because a hammer may slip when one's thumb is numb with cold. If you have any lingering mistrust of the hammerless, then get one with an automatic safety. This is an especially admirable contrivance to have on " the other fellow's " gun.

Some shotguns are locked shut by a bolt which engages lugs under the barrel. Such a mechanism is bound to wear shaky in time. There are guns of this kind so well made that they remain tight for a long period, but the principle is faulty in itself. The locking point should be as far as practicable from the hinge; as anyone can realize if he stops to think about it. The proper place is where the rearward extension of the rib enters the frame. The best fastening is a rotary bolt, which is beveled or tapered. This bolt goes from one side of the frame, through the extension rib, into the opposite side, and also locks over the extension. It is actuated by a heavy spring. Its taper automatically takes up all wear. There can be no more play than with a wedge driven home. The gun will always close tight, no matter how much it has been used.

SPORTING FIREARMS

A self-ejector is such a positive advantage on any gun that it should be applied, as a matter of course, to all but the very cheapest grades. There is no good reason why it should add more than ten dollars to the cost of the ordinary double-barrel.

As for engraving on a gun, I have already expressed the opinion that it is ornament out of place. If you must have it, then, by all means, get a pattern designed by somebody who knows art from filigree. A profusion of meaningless scrolls, or other rococo, cheapens a weapon and provides just so many extra nests for rust to breed in. Anyway, if you can afford engraving, you can afford something distinctive—a bit more original than the everlasting pointer dog or the stag at bay. Your own monogram is the best design of all.

What has been said of wood for rifle stocks applies equally to shotguns. The right fit and "hang" of a shotgun are another matter, because the arm is handled differently from a rifle. A gunner's eye, and his whole attention, should be on the mark alone. He should not be conscious of seeing either the front sight or the rib. The gun-pointing is done with his two hands, as quickly as he would point a forefinger. Hence

MECHANISM AND BUILD

the gun, to be a fit, must come up naturally, with rib parallel to line of aim (or, rather, tilted a little upward) and aligned with it, whenever the two hands are leveled on the mark.

If a gunstock is too crooked for your own build, you will shoot low; if too straight, you will overshoot. Moreover, if your cheek does not come just right against the comb of stock, you will aim diagonally across the gun's rib, without knowing it, and so shoot to right or left, as the case may be. If the heel of the stock does not rest against the same part of the shoulder, every time, your shooting will be irregular. A grip that does not fit the right hand prevents the firm grasp that is necessary to take up recoil, and so will provoke flinching. A forearm that misfits will balk a man in guiding the gun. If the stock is too short, it will buffet your face, and shoot low or in front; if too long, it will catch under your armpit, interfere with your trigger-reach, and make you shoot high and behind.

It is customary, in ordering guns, to specify only three measurements of stock, namely: the length from front trigger to center of butt, the drop at comb, and the drop at heel. These may suffice for average men, but if one is particular about getting a perfect fit, and is willing to pay

SPORTING FIREARMS

extra for it, he should give more detailed measurements, as shown in the following cut.—

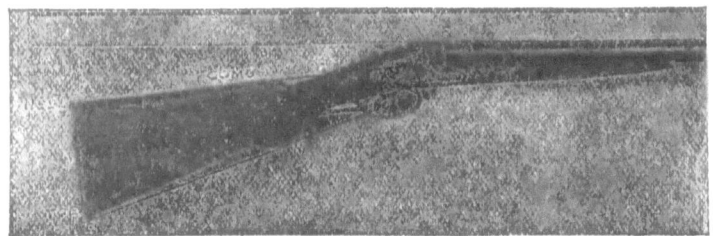

GUNSTOCK MEASUREMENTS.

First, lay a gun that fits you (or nearly fits you) on a table; then take a straight-edge as long as the gun and lay it along the top of the rib and out over the butt, snug against muzzle and breech. Now measure, as shown below, to whatever dimensions you deem best. By way of illustration I append actual measurements for a man of medium and symmetrical build.—

A-C.	Length from heel to trigger	14 5-16	inches
D-C.	Length from hollow to trigger	14¼	"
E.C.	Length from toe to trigger	14¾	"
B-B.	Drop at comb	1½	"
A-A.	Drop at heel	2½	"
A-E.	Depth from toe to heel	5⅜	"
B.F.	Length of grip	7	"
G.	Circumference of grip	4¼	"
C-H.	Trigger to cap of pistol grip	4¼	"
	Cast-off (explained below)	¼	"

In testing for length, it is important to hold the left hand in its most comfortable and master-

MECHANISM AND BUILD

ful position, well forward of the trigger guard, so as to give good command of the gun in any attitude, and yet not far enough to put any strain on the left arm. The closer one holds to the trigger guard with his left hand, the longer the stock should be, and *vice versa*. It is the left arm that really governs the proper length of stock, rather than the right.

A short-armed man requires about a fourteen-inch stock; a long-armed one, fourteen and one-half to fourteen and three-fourths. Bend of stock depends upon length of one's neck, and also upon whether he crooks his neck a good deal, in aiming, or points his gun when his head is more erect. In general, it is best to select a rather straight stock, for the express purpose of throwing the shots a little high. Most birds are shot on the rise, and all shot drops in its flight.

A full-chested man requires more hollow in the butt-plate than a flat-chested one.

The comb of a gun affects aim both vertically and horizontally. If its drop is just right for the individual user it will direct his shot at the right elevation—the comb is, in effect, a shotgun's rear sight. If its thickness just suits the shooter's face, then his eye will naturally follow the center of the gun's rib. In trying guns for drop, hold your head well up, just as you would in the field—don't sight down along the rib. Drop at heel, as a rule, is proportional to drop at comb. The usual ratios are: one and one-fourth inch at comb to two inches at heel (short neck); one and three-eighths, two and one-fourth; one and one-half, two and one-half (medium neck); one and five-eighths, two and five-eighths; one and three-fourths, two and three-fourths (long neck); one and seven-eighths, three inches.

If a pistol grip is wanted, let it be of shorter radius (four to four and one-fourth inches) and fuller curve than the present fashion. I can see no advantage in a pistol grip unless the gun has only a single trigger.

Circumference of grip is governed by the size of one's hand. A grip that is too slender cramps the hand, or slips through it when recoiling, and is easily broken in the field.

Cast-off means a sidewise bend of the stock to bring the rib into accurate alignment with the eye. A hollowed-out comb has the same effect as a cast-off to the right. Either of them helps in difficult swinging shots. The amount of cast-off, or shape of comb, is wholly dependent on one's personal build. For average men, a cast-

MECHANISM AND BUILD

off of one-eighth to three-sixteenth inch is sufficient. If you are broad-chested, more may be needed.

A gun balances right when its weight is concentrated near its center of gravity, and when this center is so placed that the right and left hands support equal weight. Such "hang" makes a gun buoyant, makes it feel lighter than it really is, and helps immensely to level the two hands when pointing for a quick shot. An ill-balanced gun is inert, sluggish in the gunner's grasp. A well-balanced one is "alive," responsive. Both weapons may be of the same weight; but one will drag and tire a man, while the other will seem a part of his very self. We all know what it means to say that "the horse and his rider are one"; in the same way should a gun and gunner be one.

THE END

www.ingramcontent.com/pod-product-compliance
Lightning Source LLC
Chambersburg PA
CBHW031115080526
44587CB00011B/978